6-09

Faces of *Alaska*

from Barrow to Wrangell

D1738855

a glimpse of history through paintings,
photographs and oral histories

by Jean Lester

First edition

Tanana Yukon Historical Society
Fairbanks, Alaska
and Poppies Publishing
Ester, Alaska

First Printing 1992
LCC No. 92-80227

ISBN 0-940457-59-8 (hardcover)
ISBN 0-940457-60-1 (softcover)

By the same author: Faces of Alaska

Book design and photographs of portraits by Jan Sanders Stitt
Photograph of Joseph E. Usibelli's portrait by Robert Usibelli
Reproduction of DeArmond's raven woodcut by permission of the artist

Printed in Singapore

Published by the Tanana Yukon Historical Society
and Poppies Publishing
P.O. Box 33
Ester, Alaska 99725

Contents

Alaska

Preface and Acknowledgements

After Faces of Alaska was published in 1988, many people asked when I was going to do another book. At the time, I said, "Never, absolutely never." But I've always wanted to see more of the state, and so after about a year, when my hair no longer stood on end and I had forgotten just how much work was really involved, I began to think of a second book. I wanted to meet people living out in some of the villages as well as in the cities and smaller towns. After many suggestions and inquiries, I settled on the places and people I've included. There are still ethnic and cultural groups and geographical areas which have not been covered, and I hope to do one more volume in this series which will include people from the areas I've missed.

While travelling about Alaska to research this book, I was often apprehensive. Sometimes I didn't know where I would be staying, or whom I would be interviewing and each place was so different. However, in every community, I met people who shared their homes, good food and wonderful conversations, and in the cases of the individuals included - also opened themselves to share their lives through this book. One of the hardest parts for me of doing the book was leaving these people. After being with them and sharing their lives, to then just step out and say, "good bye" was very difficult. They enriched my life and all became my friends.

Oral history has always had a special appeal for me. It is like a personal conversation. And it is that quality that I have tried to maintain. Our story is all we really have and by sharing it and reading about that of others, we can gain a perspective and understanding that can help us treat each other with more dignity, kindness and respect.

While interviewing, I let the individuals follow their own lead in what they want to say, rather than insist they fit into any framework. I feel the interview captures more of an individual if they talk about the topics significant to them. I have again chosen to leave out my questions. Rachel Craig, after reviewing her oral history, wrote "Jeannie - where are all the wonderful questions that elicited this verbage?" But with Rachel, and so many others, there was so much of what they said that I wanted to include, that with the space limitations involved, my choice was to keep as many of their words as possible and leave out my questions.

Most of the paintings were done very quickly, often in marginal, changing light. Many are more quick sketches than finished portraits.

Many, many people contributed to this book with their suggestions and their time. Their unhesitating help embodies what I think of as the true "spirit of Alaska." To all those who helped me - answered my many phone calls and letters, supported me and kept me going when things really didn't look like they were going to work - I thank you. I would like to decorate you with garlands of flowers. And I especially include those whom I painted and interviewed.

I am grateful to the Tanana Yukon Historical Society and the Alaska Humanities Forum for providing the major financial support for the travel and research, with the help of MarkAir, BP Exploration, the Skinner Foundation, and Edith Bullock. My thanks to Marge Naylor and David Hales in Archives and William Schneider of the Oral History Department at the University of Alaska Fairbanks; to Sally Collins for all her research and support, to Mary Lee Guthrie for frequently reminding me that the world wants quality and beauty; to Suzann Suzawith and Sue Cooper, who transcribed the many, many tapes and typed and retyped; to Jan Stitt for taking the manuscript and photos and creating a book; to Maria Brooks for her essential insights; to Mary Calmes, Father Louis Renner and Jane Williams for their guidance; to my editor Maureen Weeks, who made me aware that one's editor truly is one's best friend; and to my husband Steve and our son Andy, who griped about my many absences but encouraged me anyway.

And a very special thanks to Rose Palmquist.

Introduction

In *Faces of Alaska*, published in 1988, Jean Lester created something entirely new, something never done before. In recent years, a new sort of biography has arisen in the form of oral history, a biography constructed from the recorded words of the subjects themselves. In Ms. Lester's works, besides adding the portraits which accompany the biographies, she has brought to these recorded lives an artist's sensitivity and the "negative capability" which Keats ascribed to Shakespeare. That is, she can remove herself with such sensitivity that the experience comes through. She has allowed the people whose faces she paints to speak of their own lives from their own perspective, giving precedence to each person's own feelings and values, taken within their own context in their own places and times in Alaska's history.

It is not, however, her openness in taking oral history which has produced a new genre of biography, but the combinations of both portrait painting and oral history with her special insight. Presenting people through painting, speech and writing, Ms. Lester intensifies their experience, running it through an added dimension. In *Faces of Alaska, from Barrow to Wrangell,* as with her first book, readers receive a sense of the past through the experiences of people who look out from the page to accompany their own words.

Ms. Lester started her professional life as a painter, and while she was painting the people whose portraits appear in the first book, she was drawn into their lives and found a way to share their stories both through paint and tape recorder. She didn't just turn the tape recorder on, but developed a rapport based on trust and respect that became a collaboration. A different interviewer would have elicited a different conversation and a different aspect of their part in Alaska's history.

I have known Ms. Lester for ten years and have come to respect the depth of her interest in people's lives, and have felt the confidence she evokes through acceptance of what people themselves want to say, what is important to them. She puts people at ease because she does not come from a superior position, does not seek to classify people in academic categories. She makes her subjects comfortable enough to share their lives as they experienced them.

I am rapidly becoming an old-timer myself, and these faces and lives in living details have given me once again a poignant taste of my own lost past.

A reader will gain insight from these lives more by simply taking them in, savoring them, than by studying them. The people whose faces and lives appear here have chosen to enter the public record in a way that will deepen and enrich the understanding of others through empathy rather than intellectual abstraction.

Doris Ann Bartlett, Ph.D.
Humanities and English Depts.
University of Alaska Fairbanks

Faces
of
Alaska
from Barrow to Wrangell

Amos Turner

McGrath - Amos died October 4, 1991. He died at home with his wife and daughter, the three of them singing the old cowboy songs he loved.

Well, maybe I should start from the start. I came to Alaska in 1937 and landed in Juneau. Juneau was pretty small at that time. In the spring I decided I'd go north. I went up to Seward and took the railroad to Fairbanks. Later I bought a lot in Anchorage and built a house but it didn't suit me there, so I sold it and come to McGrath where I've been ever since. Up here I never go and open the door unless somebody can't hear. I just holler, "Come in." I figure that's the way people ought to be. That's why I like it out here. There's still a lot of the old spirit around if you just look.

Of course, over here I've done a little of almost everything - but hunting and trapping, that's my big thing. I had traps out and would pick up a few furs. Gets in your blood, that's all. You come to one trap and maybe you got something and then you wonder if you got something in the next one. It keeps you a'goin' and a'guessin'. If you're lucky you've got one in every trap, but that's very, very rare.

I had a steady job. I worked for Alaska Airlines pretty near fifteen years, and with Consolidated and BLM. I was always with the airlines wherever I went; always ended up loading and unloading airplanes. Especially in Galena during the war. The Russians were flying big planes across Alaska over to the war front and they were stopping in there. Of course a DC-3 was a huge plane then and the DC-6 was the biggest. I loaded those old Pilgrims hundreds of time. McGrath was only a hundred people then, counting the kids and maybe a dog or two.

Then I retired because of terrible shape with arthritis. But I got over ninety percent of it so I had to get on them there river boats and put in a couple of years. I was fireman on the old *Langley* and *Northwestern* riverboats. Specially coming upriver, you never leave the fire box. Six hours on and you was right there all the time. You got the water gauges, steam pressure, and you got to keep them all at a certain point if you want to get really moving. And you got to know how to put that wood in there so you can get more heat out of it. There's a

Riverboat in McGrath
Photo by Helen Teeter

trick in that. Those were four-foot sticks we put in. I sure developed some muscles in my arms and shoulders. That was about forty years ago. They'd bring in a year's supply of gas for the planes on the boats in barrels. Talk about a hazard. You get some terrible sparks going up the stack. Then if you've got a tail wind, all them sparks are flying up there around the gas barrels. Of course, the pilot house is right up above the boilers. I'm sure the captain got nervous a time or two.

Then after I retired I run my own boat, hauling freight all over, from here to Sterling, down to Devils Elbow, Takotna, Medfra, Nikolai. Some of them runs took terrible long times. I was freighting ten to fifteen years or more. I still do. I can't load or unload, but I can still take it. Now come freezeup, lot of people in town won't go out on the river until they see me go across. If I think it's the least bit bad, I'll tell 'em. I don't like to see people drown. I chop every so often to see how thick the ice is. If you hit that ice and it sounds hollow, you better back up quick.

I've done a lot of hunting and fishing while I was bringing in wrecked airplanes. I've been out on so many crews to get to the crashes. I'm not always the first one on the river or at the scene after a plane accident, but I'm not far behind. Somebody has to do it. Until somebody goes and investigates, you never know, there might be some survivors.

I've trapped ever since I was ten years old. I just loved doing that kind of thing. I've even taken a skunk out of a trap without getting sprayed. That was in Amboy, Washington. I've taken a live beaver out of a fish net he was wound up in, no gloves, no nothing. You got to know what you're doing; one slice of those teeth and he'd take your hand off. There's a lot of things you can do if you understand the animal, but if you don't and you get excited or you're in a hurry,

Amos Turner

4

Amos Turner and Forest "Tex" Gates discuss the current warm spell in the April weather
Photo by S. Collins

don't try it. Then you take wolves howling. I've never run into anyone that tried to imitate them, but I can, and have them answer to me as long as I want to. They stayed their distance but they knew right where I was at and I knew where they were.

I was born and raised among cattle and horses. There wasn't a cow I couldn't milk or a bull I couldn't ride. Of course, I got plastered up a time or two, broken bones here and there, so I quit that career and come north.

Well, I was trapping down here and doing pretty good. In the fall, I'd go in on a pontoon ship and then come out again in spring before breakup. Always tell the pilot, but you better tell someone else too, because sometimes the pilot forgets.

Once I come out loaded with nothing but wolf pelts and the same thing one time with lynx. Them wolves, you never can depend on what they're going to do when you walk up. One guy maybe can walk right up and they'll greet him like a pet dog, begging him to take the trap off. Another guy walks up and they go completely kezerky. One day I set a wolf trap and had a real long chain and wire hook up. In the morning I went down with a flashlight and seen a lot of little tracks and thought I got a fox. So I go down and see where this chain goes into a barrel. I just go end over end pulling this chain, expecting to see Mr. Fox and out come a long leg. I thought, "Oh, oh, this is the wrong church for me." That leg belonged to a wolf instead of a fox so I postponed fooling with him 'til daylight.

There's a lot of bears up in that country too, and there's grizzlies up on the Takotna River. Them bloomin' bears. I've had a lot of fun with them. Once, up at my cabin during the night, I just had to get up and head out to the bathroom. It had been raining terrible and I opened the door and one whiff of that air and I

Amos Turner

5

Plane in front of the McGrath Road House
From the Ward Wells Collection of the Anchorage Museum
of History and Art

was back in the cabin. That dad gum bear had been sleeping just on the other side of that door. He'd come in where it was dry. When I was getting the door open he'd come to and sneaked out. I'm sure glad he did. That sure scared the heck out of me. That learned me a lesson. Always take a flashlight and always take a gun with you whenever you go out, especially at night.

Once I was in a real picklement. I was going up river and I got a couple of ducks. I stopped at a nice bank and cleaned them. Then I went on moose hunting and when I come back there was a bear there. Well, I was going to camp there, it's a nice camping area. So I shot at the bear and knocked him against the bank. Well, he got up and in one jump he was in the brush and like a dummy I decided I'd go in there too. I knew he was hit bad and I figured I could finish him off so he wouldn't lay around or come back. Well, I got too far from him and I heard him between me and the boat. And it was dark by that time. Now that gives you a terrible feeling. This bear growling, and you can't see nothing. But I had to get back to the boat. So I figured there was only one way. I could hear him, so I figured I'd go direct to him and then I'd know exactly where he was at. I finally located him and killed him. He was down and couldn't get up, which I was hoping, and I was right.

I had the record of turning out some mighty fine beaver hides. It takes a lot of patience. Years ago, you had your trap line and nobody goes on it. There was an old saying that you catch a guy trapping your beavers you just make a bigger hole and wait for him and then you shoot him and shove him down that hole. Everybody respected the other guy's line in the early days. At least ninety-nine percent of them. Now you have a lot of ninety-day wonders. You wonder if they're trappers or what they are. Plain trap thieves. A lot of them around.

As soon as I stayed here for the summer I had a garden. Experimental, a lot of it. Lot of people didn't think they could raise this or that and that was about the surest way to get me to plant it. I had bees for about three or four years and got some pretty good honey. I'm a nut for honey.

If you get out there on the water, say on a real calm day with the sun shining, you get to see everything. Sometimes I shut the engine off and drift for

Amos Turner

6

hours. You might pass a beaver within a foot or closer. One time I was sleeping, and all of a sudden I heard this here scratching on the gunnels of the boat. The first thing that flashed in my mind was bear and I was in a terrible position. But up there on the gunnels of the boat was the prettiest mink you ever seen. He finally jumped down and swam to shore. He was the biggest mink I'd ever seen on the Takotna River.

You can have a real field day just watching and taking your time. There's always geese up by my old hunting cabin, right on the lake. Whole families of them. Them little guys are a'goin' and they ain't no bigger than a peanut. That's what makes a trip worthwhile.

One guy here wanted to go moose hunting with me. I promised him that I would take him and then one day he was talking about shooting swallows with a big rifle. Then he got talking about how to hunt moose. He says when you see the brush move, you shoot. I told him, "You and I will never be in the same boat and I hope we're never on the same river. If the brush is moving and you're out hunting and that brush happens to be me, you better kill me on the first shot, or I'm going to blow you right out of that boat." You never know what's going on when you see the brush move. It could be anything, often it's another person. When I shoot I want to know exactly what I'm shooting at and if at all possible I want to make a clean kill.

One thing I know now about animals, after you've been in among them for awhile, every one of them is different. You can pick out any one of them. You can almost read what they're thinking if you've been among them long enough.

Year 'round I hunt. Out of season I just like to go out and look at the animals. You can always learn something if you're willing to look and study it. I've told everybody, each time I get loose in that boat, I'm hunting. Not to kill, except a bull in the moose season - if I have any chance at all I'll get him. But otherwise, you see cow and calf and young bulls, old ones, and you get to know a lot of them by sight. I'm hunting to know them, just to see them.

If you can't eat it, don't kill it. It isn't the law or anything, it's just what you believe in. If you don't want to eat, why kill it? A lot of people all they can think of is kill. Sufferin' horntoads, there's no sense in it. There's more of that there killing nowadays. Several times I've found beaver dead, floating in the river, shot. And that's a dirty crime. But some people don't look at it that way. They see it as a target. But if you want a target, put up a tin can. There's always something you can shoot at that ain't going to hurt nothing or nobody.

Amos Turner

7

Margaret Calvin

Sitka - Margaret speaks and moves quickly as she takes me down a long path through the woods to the print shop. When she starts the printing machine - bent over from osteoporosis and with her white hair and bright blue eyes - I feel I am watching an elf printing a fairy tale.

I was a physical therapist in an army general hospital unit in Texas during World War II, and patients who had been on the Aleutian campaign raved about Alaska. So later, when I was living in the middle of Chicago, I wrote to every hospital in Alaska asking if they needed a physical therapist. The answer was "no" except for a letter from the then Territory of Alaska that said they were thinking of opening a children's orthopedic hospital because tuberculosis of the bone was so rampant in Alaska at that time, and that they would keep my letter on file. Well, I just kind of gave up on the whole idea. But six months later, I got a letter saying their hospital was materializing. And so on May 30, 1947, I landed in Sitka. I like to think that I was probably the first physical therapist in Alaska.

When I first came, we weren't terribly busy a lot of the time, so I would help out in surgery by doing cleanup or I would go into the wards and feed the children. But soon they got more patients and I was quite busy. It was a very well-equipped department.

Sitka was definitely a very small town at that time, less than half the size it is now, three thousand people at the very most. A fishing village, really, with gravel roads that led out to Sawmill Creek, because there had been a sawmill out that way at one time, and to Halibut Point. We could walk the beaches and probably some of my happiest memories of that time are the Sunday afternoon walks out Halibut Point Road, picking berries and combing the beaches for shells. Now there are homes all along that area and you would be walking in front of somebody's private property. Although the beaches are public property, you still don't do that sort of thing. Totem Park was here - it is really the Sitka Historic National Park - and we had lots of picnics on the beach there, too, whereas now they don't allow you to build a fire on the beach.

Mount Edgecumbe had been a navy base during World War II and

Sitka, Alaska
The Photo Shop Studio

developed into the hospital unit and also a school for Native children. When I first arrived, in order to get into Sitka and do your shopping you had to climb onto a small shoreboat, which ran back and forth across the channel between the Mount Edgecumbe installation and the Sitka town every half hour, no matter what the weather.

I loved it, I guess, from the very first. I settled here, married and had two children, raised them, and am still here.

When my children were college age, my first husband and I were divorced. I had an old family friend - he and his wife had been my friends all the time I had been in Sitka - and when she died, he came courting. We married. He had been the town printer for many, many years and had retired. But he decided he would like to have a print shop - no deadlines, no commercial printing - just little books with an Alaskan theme. I didn't know the first thing about printing, but we built the shop and equipped it. However, it was not without some difficulties since the shop was located on the beach with access only by water or down a quarter-mile trail. The equipment was all second hand but Jack knew where to go to ferret it out. He wanted to get back to the hands-on letterpress way of doing things wherein you take each letter of type and set it, composing the whole page letter by letter. After you have printed it, you break the type down into the individual pieces and put them back in the case. So, if you want to do that page again, you have to start back at the beginning.

He was a great teacher and the first book he wanted to do was a little short history of Sitka, which he had written and printed many years before when he was in the printing business. So, he set the type and I was the printer's devil and got ink on my fingers. It soon "gets into your blood" and you can't help but be a printer from there on in.

I like it because it's a hands-on type of thing. There has been quite a resurgence in letterpress printing as a craft or as an art form. Just before the Sitka book was all set and ready to be put out on the market, Jack had a stroke. So he was out of the picture, which meant that either I tried to continue, or gave up. As I have said many times before, not knowing what you don't know, you carry on. So I just dove in - I thought I knew all about it, you know. I'd had the ten happiest years of my life with Jack. He left me with the printing business,

Margaret Calvin
10

which gives me goals in my old age. And because there are no deadlines, I can do it when I want to. Every time you produce a book, it is like you have developed a child because a lot of you has gone into it. And people buy it. They actually buy it! But I would hate to have to live on the money I make selling books.

I had challenges all along the way and had some wonderful help from local people who did know about letterpress printing. Working with Dale DeArmond while printing her books has developed a relationship that has been wonderful for me. She had lived in Sitka and I had known her before they moved to Juneau, so she was a friend before we started working together.

I knew when I went to college that I wanted to do something in the medical world, either a lab technician or a physical therapist or a dental assistant. I chose physical therapy because my Aunt Gertrude was a physical therapist and I had been around her as I grew up. I am sure that she had a great influence on me. She was a single person, known as an "old maid" in those days, and she loved to travel. She considered my sister and me as her foster children and would take us on long driving trips out West. She opened my eyes to other parts of the world aside from the middle class, Midwest America in which I had grown up. It gave me the desire to join the army in World War II and I was in the army medical corps as a physical therapist, eventually going to England. Aunt Gertrude was a person who always knew what to give a child for Christmas - the exact thing that you wanted.

Sitka, Alaska
August 1947
The Photo Shop Studio

Margaret Calvin

11

Of course, my family were very instrumental because they led me down the right paths. We had some good upbringing with rules of the house, which we maintained. Much of my childhood was spent during the Depression and it's a great boon to me in this day of recycling and reusing. I find it's an asset to have had that background of not wasting.

There certainly was no doubt in any of our minds as children but that we would go to college. It had been one of my father's goals in life to see to it that his children had college educations.

I had a good friend in high school whose family was very outdoorsy. They went to Colorado every year and went to a cabin and roughed it, climbing and hiking and all sorts of things. My family was not that sort. They were not outdoorsy. They never went on a camping trip, ever.

When I was choosing a college, I chose the University of Colorado just because this friend of mine was going there. That's where I really learned about the great outdoors. It certainly had an influence on my desire to come to Alaska. We skied, hiked, camped, rented cabins in the woods for weekends and took long drives up into the mountains. That was certainly my exposure to the great outdoors.

As a child I never went out and picked berries. We never canned things, and so here in Alaska I have twenty-seven years of gathering to make up for. I just love to get out and pick berries, freeze them or make jams and wines, and to make kelp pickles and Sitka spruce-tip syrup. And some of it I give for Christmas gifts to my family down in the States. I should send them a blouse that they can get cheaper and better down there?

Jack was one of the very early conservationists and a charter member of the Sitka Conservation Society. Through his efforts and those of other people, an area just north of here was designated the first citizen-originated national wilderness area.

One of the important things in my life is a group of friends here in Sitka, which we call our "extended family" and which has been very close. It consists of about five families. We celebrate Thanksgiving, New Year and Christmas together. It's a family, in effect, and it certainly is special in my life.

I 'hink of myself as being able to do most everything I set my mind to, so long as it is within my physical strength and there are instructions written about it. I have tackled things on that basis and I think Alaska has brought out my confidence in myself. You just have to be a little more self-reliant - you've got to kind of figure out what makes things work so you can fix it. Then you are more confident to do the next thing.

Margaret Calvin

12

Margaret and Jack Calvin
Collection of Margaret Calvin

I worked as a physical therapist until just before my son was born in 1949. But in the early 50s, when finances dictated it, I started to work at the city offices and spent the next twenty-eight years there. I started out in a clerical position but rose to city clerk and later finance director. They were rewarding years and I like to think I had some influence in making Sitka a better place to live. The town doubled in size during that time and there were always new challenges.

Absolutely the worst period of my life was when my osteoporosis came to a head about six years ago and I was having collapses of the vertebrae about once a month. I sort of pride myself in being able to take pain, but when one of these vertebrae would collapse ("spontaneous" is what they call it - you don't do anything, it just happens), talk about pain! It was incredible, and I would be practically bedridden for a few days. I would slowly get up, but every now and then it would catch and I would just stand there in excruciating pain. It would slowly get better and better and about a month after it happened I would be able to function again. And then another one would break. This went

Margaret Calvin

Sitka, Alaska
Collection of The Photo Shop

on for about six or eight months, about one a month, and it was so excruciating that I even considered suicide. I went so far as to write a suicide note to my family one morning. Probably the only thing that kept me from it, maybe, was the fact that I didn't know how to go about it.

Osteoporosis is primarily a feminine disease and doctors are mostly men and they don't pay any attention to it. My message to the world is that I am living proof that osteoporosis is reversible. It is just a case of finding the right doctor. When I first had a CAT scan, my bone mass in my vertebrae was about twenty percent of normal. A year later it was forty percent of normal. In other words, I had doubled my bone mass. The next year it was fifty percent of normal and it has leveled off at fifty to sixty percent, which my doctor says is fine.

I broke my hip a year and a half ago. There was no doubt in my mind from the very beginning but what I was going to recover. Yet in later reading, I find that about twenty-five percent of people my age who break their hips, die, and of those remaining, fifty percent of them turn out with some disability. I really

Margaret Calvin

14

think my physical therapy background had a great deal to do with it. I knew what to do. I was in good shape when it happened, I had done a lot of walking and swimming. I am now back to about ninety-seven percent of what I was before. I think the essential thing is that there wasn't any doubt in my mind but what I was going to do it. There are too many things in the world to do to give up. The world is so full of things to know and to learn and to do. I have some more books to put out and even if I can't print after one of these years, think of all the good organizations in town that need your help; it's endless. If nothing else, you can go to the Pioneers' Home and read to the pioneers who can't read. I know a lot of young people who do that but you don't have to be young to do it.

I recently got into recycling and waste reduction here in Sitka. I have been active in the conservation movement here for a long time and even was president of the Southeast Alaska Conservation Council for a period of time. But it was a frustrating business because you were dealing with people in Washington, legislators and people in Juneau that you couldn't really feel like you were influencing. So when the subject of recycling came up in Sitka, I thought, "That's what I've been waiting for. Garbage is something I can see, I can feel. It's an understandable subject to the common man." So when the city set up an ad hoc committee to deal with its solid wastes, I thought that my knowledge of municipal ways might come in handy and I applied for a position. And now I'm up to my chin in garbage day after day after day.

I've had two children, both of whom have turned out well and have careers, which are useful to mankind and humanity, who married people I think the world of and have given me grandchildren that are the apples of my eye. How much luckier can you get?

And I'm very grateful to the Calvin family for having embraced me and my family as they did because I certainly came into their lives late. All of Jack's family have been very open and have been equally open to my children and their offspring. That is certainly a very nice thing to have happened to me. Many people over the years have been very kind to me. Often I cannot repay those people directly. The only way I can possibly repay them is to do something good for other people. And I try to do that.

Just as fate had a hand in bringing me to Sitka, I think sometimes we have to let fate decide what we are going to do. We may come to a parting in the road and if we just lay back, and don't push it, something will happen to tell us which way to go.

Margaret Calvin

Albert A. Zucchini

Ester - Al is loved by the Ester community where he is seen walking wherever he needs to go. He's all of about four feet, eight inches, and laughs as he tells people his name is "Big Al." His cabin is sparse - a stove, a bed, a table and a good mug of tea.

Well, here I am at seventy-nine years young, having forty-one good years in Alaska, continuous.

I was raised in St. Louis, Missouri, and had very little schooling. I had one brother and three sisters and have survived them all. But our financial situation was low, low. I was by far the youngest in the family. My dad passed away before I was old enough to go to grammar school so in a way it was kind of hard times. There was enough, but there wasn't any excess. So I was left on my own pretty much of the time, since my sister and my mother had to provide for the food and everything else that goes with it.

So eventually I drifted around and got into travelling various places in the Lower 48. I always was willing to work for unskilled labor and to make a small amount to get by. So I drifted here and there finding something to do. It was never any problem. Then there was World War II and like all Americans, I wanted to do something so I became a seaman. I had about two years on the seas on tankers as it was, travelling in the Pacific mainly. But as a seaman, I was continuously at sea and never at any one place any length of time. Stays ashore in Australia, the Philippines, India, or Iran, wherever it might be, were very short. So I can say I've been there, but in actuality, I never knew anything really about these foreign places that I'd been.

Well, anyway, when all the hostilities was over and peace was made, I no longer cared for a life at sea. I'm what you call a land lover. So my life as a seaman terminated in California and I stayed there until August 1947. Meanwhile, I'd been reading and was intrigued by the life of mining people. I'd previously had a little experience mining in Nevada, and I was fascinated by that and, of course, as a younger person, maybe getting rich overnight had a strong appeal. But then, being with the miners, outdoor life, being close to nature, often in remote areas, also had a strong appeal. More and more I became

Albert Zucchini's home in Ester
Jan Stitt photo

Al Zucchini
Steve Lester photo

interested in what Alaska was like. So eventually I got up to Seattle and I had saved a few pennies and I got on the airplane on August 3, 1947.

Well, on arriving at Fairbanks there was a lot of activity. They were constructing what is now Eielson Air Force Base and they were improving what is now Fort Wainwright. It was called Ladd Field then. Anyway, in the course of this I had to have employment, which was very easy to obtain at that time. I done various things, working in construction. Now war surplus was very plentiful for a few years. Not too long after I come up here I met a fine man. Mr. Justice has now left this world a long time ago, but he was very apt with dealing with people and supplying a need no matter what it might be, a used article or a new article. He had that touch of dealing with people and sensing what a value might be on something. Amazing as I recall it. So I got to be his right-hand man and we were handling a lot of war surplus. And, of course, a little of that rubbed off on me and eventually I could follow in the same pattern. And I bought a lot of surplus, a world of it, and worked in surplus until Mr. Justice died. From then on, one thing led to another, and I drifted into the thing that really brought me up into the country - mining.

The freedom, the independence, the fact that minerals come from Mother Nature - there's an attraction to a lot of men and it certainly attracted me. I just felt at home in the woods. To be successful, like anything, you have to put a lot of effort into it and where mining's concerned, it's plenty of hard work. Lots of hard physical labor. And you never get it out of your system once you acquire it. Even today, at my age, I'm still vitally interested in mining and mining people. And whether you like it or not, gold today is like it was five thousand years ago.

Albert A. Zucchini

18

The Steese Highway in Fairbanks, Alaska. Circa 1940
Collection of the Stitt family

We all know it would be pretty hard to exist without money under any circumstances.

Like I said. I tried various ways to make a living which was never any problem because I always had the right attitude about working. Everybody's got to work. It's still my version about living, you've got to contribute to society. If you get the benefits, you've got to contribute, which I did.

Meanwhile, I spent considerable time with a man called Earl Hurst. He was considerably older than me at the time. He himself had spent practically all of his life in the bush and from him I learned so much about living in the woods. I've been with Hurst all over and his experience of a lifetime of hunting, trapping and mining done a wonderful thing for me. Not only that, but I'm happy to say he was one of the finest characters I ever met. Trustworthy and responsible, willing, and a nature that was just ideal. He had a marvellous personality. I learned so much of what I think I know today of how to survive in remote areas.

If you've spent so much time under conditions that aren't exactly easy living, you appreciate little things. This man Hurst was an excellent hunter and could almost live off the country. You learn these things. They seem so easy to talk about but they take some doing to live through. And in the course of this, it tears up your life, makes you independent and you get to the point, even where I am now, that I think of myself as too independent. And you can't be. We're in a society and you have obligations and you got to think of the other guy, the other person, other family. I regret that I never was married.

I met so many mining people because I singled mining people out as the people I was most interested in. I can recall being with Sam Gamblin, who was a man pretty much to my nature, loved to travel all over Alaska. Just a lover of nature you might call him, just being satisfied to be out in nature's environment, remote places. There's ever so many old miners that I've been with but basically they were men of good character regardless of what their financial was, which really doesn't mean anything when you're out in bush areas.

I've always had a fondness of hiking, particularly out in bush country. I can hike anywhere. I just got into the hiking habit and miles and distances. It never has been anything but a good thing in my life.

Albert A. Zucchini

19

Mining never was too lucrative but it was a very satisfying way of life. Placer mining, as we call it, involves hard work. As time went on I got a little more involved, so a great part of my time was in interior Alaska, remote at times.

I can recall at least two times where, frankly, I was totally lost. In fact, on one occasion I was so totally lost that I thought that it was the end. Very few people might have experienced being lost to the total that you ask, "Where do I go from here?" Then as a Christian you wonder if you are going to be rewarded for living as you have. So, anyway, I did reach that point where I just gave up hope. And, by the way, when you're totally lost to that degree, it's hard to describe what happens to your mental then. It's impossible to put it into words. You have no hope. You're just up against a blank wall and you wonder, "What's my end?" However, I did recover a little bit to do something. Somehow or another I picked up the thought that if I got up into a very high elevation, maybe it might change something. I was a couple of hundred miles north of Fairbanks, out in the Bush in the middle of nowhere, no human within fifty or seventy-five miles. So in getting up on the highest elevation I was able to recognize something about landmarks in the far distance that was familiar. There again, it's very difficult to describe the relief and thankfulness that came to me at that point. I was more thankful at that moment than I ever was in my life.

Meanwhile, in years gone by I acquired a little land here in Ester. I always thought it was important to own a piece of land or to have something you worked for. That was one of my first objectives when I come to Alaska. At that time, of course, values and money and finances were entirely different. So I managed with very little money to start buying a place to live. The fact that there were mining claims is what attracted me to this property out here. This has always been a historical area as far as mining is concerned and goes way back. I've found Ester a very happy little community and people cooperating and respecting others and just enjoying the good life here. I really don't know of any place that would fill my life like the simple living that I have out here.

So as time goes on and a guy gets a few years on him he thinks more seriously. With age, your mind turns to things that you might have overlooked in your younger life. Things that you walked right by and you never gave any attention to because they never appeared to be that important. Or not important. What now appears to be the most important things, I didn't recognize then. I wonder about my sanity that I went by these things that now appear to be the most important things in the world -- to be compatible with the world we live in, and to make a contribution to return what has been provided to everyone, and to make a good contribution to the young people.

Albert A. Zucchini

20

You get to be a philosopher, I guess. You ask yourself a little bit about life. Where are you? Who are you? Things like this. So there's a lot of unanswered questions and at my age I don't expect to come up with answers on many things. In some ways, life is a riddle. However, I always was raised as a Christian and I've never lost it and I never will, I'm sure of that. This is important to a man's life. I just can't imagine how a man can live in society and on this earth and not have convictions on his spirit, on his living, on his relation to God, we'll say. Incidentally, I've become in these years of learning, appreciative of what our forefathers did, allowing everybody to worship as they wished, and freedom of the press. To me those are the greatest things that Americans can be thankful for. And I'm thankful, very thankful.

Incidentally I was very fortunate that my health was pretty good all the way, I feel that I've been more fortunate than the average person might be.

There was never a time when I didn't appreciate other people. Of course, due to very little education or schooling, I had to rely on physical strength and will power to exist. I feel that I've been very favored. I can't think of anyone that I think is more fortunate than I am, whether it's financial or spiritual or otherwise. So I think I've made the grade. And after all these years and so long in Alaska I pass on the reminder that the gold, the money and the possessions are not what makes people. It's the trials of life, the willingness to accept the obligation to their fellow man and society. If you do this, you've done your job.

Celebrating the Fourth of July on Cushman Street in Fairbanks, Alaska. circa 1940
Collection of the Stitt family

Dale DeArmond

Juneau - The gentle light from her window reflects on her as she works at her kitchen table, often glancing up as we laugh and talk of our lives as women and artists. [The DeArmonds moved to Sitka in 1990].

My great-grandmother came from Ireland during one of the many times of trouble. The family story is that she went home one day and found her father hung by the neck from the door frame. She was seventeen years old, and she fled with her ten year old nephew. Somehow they made their way to America. She married a man who took her to the Dakota Territories, and she is said to have raised nineteen children. Probably her husband had been married before and some of the children were from that marriage. By the time I knew her - I was seven years old when she died - she wasn't much bigger than I was. She smoked a clay pipe, as many country Irish women did. Great-grandmother raised her family in North Dakota, and my parents were both born and grew up there, and I was born there.

My father was very active in radio when it was first starting. He worked for the Bell Telephone Company and had a gift for electronics. I can remember sitting on the floor of the house in St. Paul, listening to a radio that he had made that was somehow connected up with a phonograph, one of those big old cabinet phonographs, and hearing distant music. There weren't many radio stations in those days, so I don't know where the music was coming from. He had been out to the West Coast in his early years as a teenager, and he'd never forgotten the salt water. So he took his family to Tacoma when I was about seven. My mother and my brother and sister and I went on the train, and I was quite fascinated with that journey. I remember the prickly green seats, the little berths that you climbed into at night, and the sound of the wheels after the lights were out.

I grew up in Tacoma, went to school there, and eventually got into radio work. I was interested in the broadcasting and writing end of it. I got started doing a children's program at one of the radio stations. I was fifteen, I think. I adapted fairy tales, and directed and produced half-hour programs, taking the

Transporting wild hay for the U.S. Department of Agriculture experiment station at Sitka, about 1904. The oven, the wagon and the scow all belonged to the station. Standing on the bow of the scow was R.W. DeArmond, horticulturalist at the experiment station.
Collection of the DeArmond family

best parts for myself, of course. That led to other things, and finally I was given my own program, writing and directing a two-person situation comedy for Buick cars. In those naive days we worked the advertising right into the play - which took some ingenuity. It was all great fun but the pay was miniscule, just about enough to pay car fare and lunch money. But I was fortunate to have any job, because this was deep into the Depression. We were luckier than many people, because my father always had a job. The Bell Telephone Company did something rather interesting when the Depression hit. Instead of laying men off, they cut everybody down to first four days, and then down to three days a week. It was enough to live on without going hungry or being desperate.

Bob and I met in a biology class in high school. We dissected a frog together. Bob had gone down to Tacoma to attend high school because the high school in Sitka wasn't accredited at that time. After he graduated and left Tacoma, we carried on a voluminous correspondence - both being people of the written word. In 1935 he was back in Sitka and invited me up for a visit. I came, fully intending to go back and have a career in radio, but of course, I didn't and we were married in July of that summer. I was twenty-one years old.

Radio at that time was pretty limited for women. You could write and do various chores, but the news desk - which was the most interesting part - was sacred to the male sex. Nowadays, of course, women can be, and are, news reporters on both radio and television. But on television the women must be

Dale DeArmond

young and good looking, while the men can be old and fat and bald, so things haven't changed that much.

I had never lived in a small town until I went to Sitka in 1935, and I was enchanted with it. I remember walking down the street for the first time and feeling that the earth was friendly there. There were only about twelve hundred people in Sitka at that time, and no one had ever heard of a chainsaw. All the roads were lined with trees and drifts of foxglove grew along the verges in the summer. Those disappeared during the war, I suspect they discovered herbicides and someone decided foxgloves were a nuisance. There were only two gasoline-driven vehicles and no telephones in Sitka in 1935.

Bob's proper field was journalism, but there weren't any newspaper jobs available, so he worked in the fish business. We stayed in Sitka for four years, and our first child was born there in 1938.

The fishermen in Sitka were discontented, as fishermen generally are, and Kalle Raatikainen proposed that they go out to Lisianski Inlet and build a town nearer to their hearts' desire. So they all went out to where Kalle had found a good townsite and built the town of Pelican. They asked Bob to come along as the accountant and business person. Bob went out to Pelican before even a tree had been cut down, and I took the baby and went down to Tacoma to visit my folks.

Unfortunately, there were two bad fishing years and the money ran out, and after five months I wrote and said I was coming up even if we had to live under a spruce tree.

Bob arranged passage on the old *Tongass*, a freighter with a few staterooms, and I packed up the baby and took off. There were twelve passengers, and we were twelve days enroute. I remember washing diapers in the hand basin and drying them in the stateroom.

In the meantime, Bob had a big sixteen by twenty foot tent put up on a wooden floor with frame walls that went part way up, and even a window. We had a big Duotherm oil range for heat and cooking, cupboards made of egg crates, a cobbled-up table, and various things to sit on. And that's where we lived, quite comfortably, for the next two years. Our second child was born while we lived in the tent. I went into Sitka for the birthing.

At the end of the second year, the Pelican cold storage was built, and we had a small apartment over the store. Bob's job had expanded, and he was the storekeeper, postmaster, steamship agent, and radioman, as well as the accountant. There were about fifty people in Pelican at that time and very little money. Fishing was bad and the price was low. Bob would send twenty-five or thirty

Dale DeArmond

25

The tent living quarters of Dale and Bob DeArmond, son William and daughter Jane during the early construction days of the cold storage plant at Pelican, 1939-40.
Collection of the DeArmond family

dollars over to Port Althorp to keep Pelican going for another few days - groceries were cheaper in those days. We ate a lot of venison and clams, goosetongue (edible seagrass) and wild berries.

I enjoyed the years in Pelican. It was an adventure and I was young and felt that I was coping. And I'm glad I had the experience. It's my insurance. I know you can get along with very few things that you generally think you need to have. And get along quite comfortably. Our big problem in Pelican was getting enough to read. Books are a major part of my life. Some have been my mentors and I know that much of my ethical sense comes from books I read as a child. Children can learn enormously from books and can enjoy very preachy books without knowing that they are preachy. They can accept preaching from books which they won't accept from Mother. One year at Christmas, Bob's folks gave us fifty dollars, which was a lot of money in those years when the average novel sold for two and a half dollars and a hardback nonfiction book would run to less than ten dollars. We invested our fifty dollars in books and started a rental library in the store. Fishermen are great readers, and the rental library was a success. We charged five cents a day and plowed the profits back into books, and had no further problem getting enough to read.

Very small towns can be difficult and Pelican was no exception. Disagreements mushroom into feuds in the long winters, and at the end of six years it was time to move on. We returned to Sitka very briefly and then a job as city editor and reporter opened up at the *Fishing News* in Ketchikan. We stayed in Ketchikan for four years. Bob worked at what soon became the *Ketchikan Daily News* and I did a woman's program at the local radio station and worked part time at the library and took care of our two kids and the house and all those good things. This was long before the feminist movement enlightened us, so my radio program ran heavily to household hints and recipes and lots of book reviews.

In 1949 we returned to Sitka and Bob went into the printing business with Jack Calvin and wrote a statewide political column for several newspapers around the state. He went to Juneau for each legislative session. And that was the time, of course, when the children got the chicken pox and measles, and the furnace quit working, and the water froze, but we all survived.

As a consequence of this political column, when Frank Heintzleman was appointed territorial governor he asked Bob to go to Juneau as an administrative assistant. We intended to stay in Juneau for four years, and stayed for thirty-eight. After the Heintzleman term ended, Bob worked as editor of the *Alaska Sportsman Magazine* and later edited the *Alaska Journal of History and Art.*

To backtrack a bit, Frank Heintzleman was very interested in libraries and when he was regional forester for Alaska, before he became governor, he had started a service that took books out to the small communities in Southeast Alaska on the Forest Service boats. They devised a crate which opened up into a double book case. And it must have been a godsend in the small towns and villages. While he was governor, Frank established the Territorial Library Service, primarily as a service to the bush and to the small libraries around the state. Dorothy Phelps was the first Territorial Librarian and because I had worked in the small libraries in Sitka and Ketchikan, I was given the job of administrative assistant. Dorothy was an old time, by-the-book librarian and working for her for three years was a full course in library science. The small libraries were mostly established and run by volunteers. They had worked very hard, and you had to tread carefully because they were very independent and not always happy to have someone who knew nothing about their struggles coming and telling them what to do and how to do it. Part of my job was to try to explain one to the other.

When the job of City Librarian opened up at the Juneau Memorial Library, I applied for it and was hired. At that time I had one half-time assistant. When I retired twenty-one years later, we had two branches and more than twenty-six people working in three libraries. Running a small public library is about as pleasant and rewarding a way to earn a living as you could find.

All my life I have made things with my hands, but I was grown, married and the mother of two children before I realized that I needed that in my life. A friend started a correspondence course in drawing and found she didn't have time for it so she turned it over to me, and I completed it. I began trying to paint and was frustrated because I didn't know enough, and finally Bob wearied of my complaining and gave me the Famous Artists correspondence course for Christmas. It was a two-year course, and they sent you four enormous and really quite wonderful loose-leaf books containing twenty-four lessons and you were supposed to complete one lesson a month. I was working and keeping a house and children and husband fed and reasonably clean, so it took me three years, but I did finish the course and got my

Dale DeArmond

certificate. I'm probably one of the few human beings who did. I really don't know how I did it now. I worked at night on the lessons. It's certainly not the ideal way to study art, but the course required a lot of work, and you can't do that much work without learning something. Their criticism was thorough and good. What it lacked was seeing technique demonstrated.

Then, in 1960, Dannie Pierce came to town and demonstrated woodcut printmaking at the annual Juneau Arts and Crafts show, and I was hooked. Dannie Pierce was at that time the visiting Carnegie professor of art at the University at Fairbanks. I was fascinated and stood there all day and watched the man do this, and went out the next morning and bought the X-acto tools - a knife and a gouge - and some wood, and scrounged some ink from the local print shop, and I was off and running. I've never gone back to painting.

Later Dannie Pierce came back to Juneau twice and taught woodcut workshops. I took both of them and learned a lot. I was very fortunate to find my medium. There is some special fascination in the repeated image, and when you print a woodcut, it's always a surprise. You don't know what it will look like till you pull up that paper from the inked block and there it is, in reverse from the way you cut it on the block and looking quite new and different. But after you've printed about six and got it just about the way you want it, it would be very nice to just forget the whole thing and not have to do the printing. I like cutting. I like the working with wood.

I remember that I was very surprised when people began to buy my work. They had started to buy my charcoal drawings and things before I went into woodcuts. But certainly Alaska is very kind to artists, because Alaskans buy a lot of Alaskan art.

I came upon the raven cycle of myths when I first went to Sitka. When I started doing woodcuts, I realized that this was the perfect medium for illustrating the raven stories. The thirty woodcuts for the raven book were my first big woodcut project and it took me two years to complete. The original stories in Swanton's *Tlingit Myths and Texts* were not meant for the general reader, and the stories needed to be retold. I rewrote them and discovered that I enjoyed doing it. Bob Henning, who was interested in ravens and in my woodcuts, agreed to publish the book through his firm, Alaska Northwest Publishing Company, and made a very handsome hardcover book of it, but it was frightfully expensive. A couple of years ago, they did a quality paperback which was really what I wanted in the first place.

Dale DeArmond

28

I hate to use the word "creative" because it has been so overused and misused but I'm sure the need to make things is indigenous to the human race. Even the most primitive people make things which have no utilitarian purpose. The impulse is non-verbal, but I think it has to do with making a record of something important to you. It's a way of honoring life and the earth.

The idea in your head is always so much better than the one you get down on paper or on canvas or whatever. So you always have something more to learn. The process is not relaxing, but there's something very healing about it. I suppose it's because you're totally concentrating on something that is outside yourself. It's not a part of any of your problems, you're just concentrating on making this thing work. You are making something.

All small children make things but the impulse is lost for most of them somewhere along the way. Those of us who never lose that impulse are the lucky ones. We have a socially acceptable way to continue to make mud pies.

In Juneau the houses really climb the hills. This is the Starr Hill section of town.
Collection of the DeArmond family

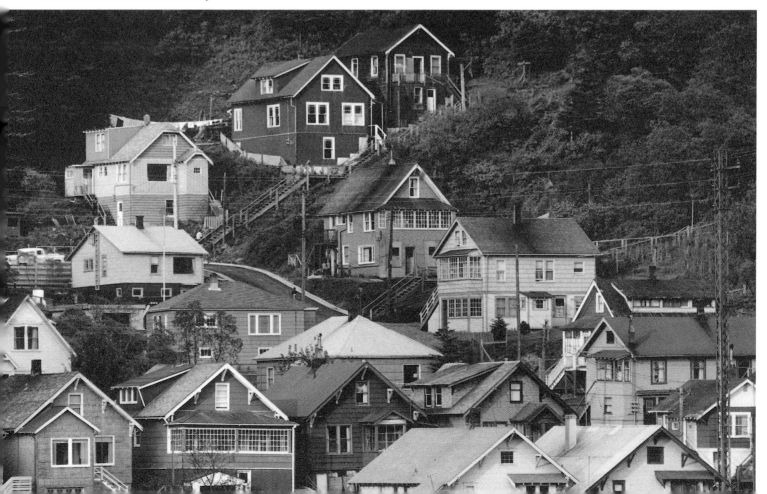

Ray Christiansen

Bethel - The flat Yukon delta is all one can see when approaching from the air. Later, Ray tells me that until only a few years before, the town was always moving with the shifting of the river, which may account for the residual restlessness I feel here.

Dad was from Larabik, Norway, and I don't know how he got over here but he was an old sailor. That was how I learned how to sail; I was weaned on a pair of oars.

I was born in Eek in 1922. Dad had a couple of sailing ships, two-masted schooners, and he also ran a trading post. Then we moved to Togiakpak and Dad started a store there. We were the only ones there. Dad always said, "People like to travel a little bit when they want to buy things." So we lived about six miles away from another village they called Kinak. There was another trader there, an old timer they called "Klondike" Johnson. They called him "Klondike" because he was up at the Klondike Mine in the old days.

My mother was an Eskimo. In the old days the natives used to fight among each other. There were people who went out from their village to other villages and fought. According to the story I have, my great-great-grandfather, my mother's great-grandfather, did that. He left the Kuskokwim area and went over to Bristol Bay where he ran in to white people. He stopped there and married. That was where my mother was born, in Bristol Bay. Evidently her parents passed away when she was very young and a Russian priest and his family adopted her. Later, the church burned down in Nushagak and the Russian priest moved to Kodiak and she went along with them. I think that is where Dad met her. That is how she got to be Russian Orthodox.

When I was about five or six years old, Dad decided to take us out to Seattle on the old *Tupper*, the old steamship. We went out and stayed all winter. Before that, Dad used to sail to Seattle to get the winter's equipment for sale at the store. This time we went out on the steamship. While we were there, he bought a boat which had a twenty horse Regal in it. He also put a mast in because dad was no mechanic, so he depended mostly on sailing. We came up through the Inside Passage with a pretty good size storm in the Gulf. It took us

about a month to come up with that boat. And that winter Dad passed away. He made a trip up to Bethel, and on his way back he froze to death. That was in 1932.

Then they sent me to school at the Moravian orphanage up in Kwethluk. Dad evidently was a Lutheran and the Moravian church is something like the Lutheran church. I grew up there until I was fifteen or sixteen years old. We didn't have high schools and we had a schoolhouse there that went from first grade all the way to the seventh all in one room. When I see the schools people have now, think they have it pretty good. Anyway, I came out of the Moravian orphanage, which was later changed to the Moravian Children's Home, and helped my sister who was taking care of the trading post after Dad died. And then I started trapping.

I would trap in the wintertime to make a living. I was too young to go fishing then as a captain or a boat puller. I was in my teens. We were down there about a year after I got out of the children's home, when an old friend of Dad's called Sam Nesvog came by and took us all over to Bristol Bay. I stayed with him for a couple of years. He had a nephew who was a pilot and had his own airplane. I used to help him cast off and warm the engine up. Later on he married my sister, Christina.

I always wanted to fly. I remember hearing about Lindbergh's flight and I often wondered how it felt. The first time I saw an airplane was when we were in Seattle, Dad took us up on a trip from Seattle to Burlington. That was my first flight - the first time I sat in an airplane. When I first saw it, it was about six or seven miles away and it looked to me like it was flopping its wings. I always thought they flopped their wings. I really did. When we lived in West Seattle, Boeing Field was next door. They used to take off and do loops and I really thought that was something. I didn't realize that I would be doing it later on.

Along about '43, they got me in the army. Of all things, I've sailed all of my life, and what did they do but put me in clinical warfare service which I didn't

*Ray Christiansen's
father, mother and
little sister in
Kwigillingok, 1913*
Collection of the
Christiansen family

know anything about. So I took my training in Anchorage and then went down to Whittier. They took us down and put us on the old troop ship *Christopher Greenup*. We went from Whittier to Adak and stayed in Adak for about two weeks because there were submarines out there. There were fourteen hundred of us and finally we went down to Attu. The fighting was just about over then so I got into the tail end. From there they moved me to Shemya and I stayed there for a couple of years.

I finally got discharged and came back to the Bristol Bay area. Then I was old enough and the people knew I could sail a boat, so the cannery let me have a boat, as a captain. My cousin, Harvey Samuelson, wanted to fish with me. It was his first year of fishing. He was very good and we were partners for four years. I was the captain and he was a boat puller. That was about '46. My brother-in-law was down in Kwigillingok running the store. I fished that summer and my brother-in-law came over to pick me up in the airplane he chartered from Northern Consolidated. On the way to Bethel, we ran out of gas and ended up in the head of Kwethluk River. We stayed there for about a week before another airplane came to pick us up and they landed on a sand bar and flipped over. I think this is what got me going on wanting to fly. We finally got out by building a little airport and someone came to pick us up with a Piper Cub. Anyway, that fall, my brother-in-law and I went out to run the Kwigillingok store. We were in our early twenties. I trapped while he was running the store. At the same time I was studying my CAR (Civil Aeronautic Rules); now they call them FAR (Federal Aeronautic Rules). This was the fall of 1946.

In 1947 I went to Anchorage to take advantage of the GI Bill of Rights to learn to fly. I got my private license and went back fishing that summer. It was a pretty good season and that fall I bought an airplane with floats, skis and wheels for twenty three hundred dollars. It was a used T-Craft, but I got my two hundred hours out of it. Then a friend of mine talked me into getting my commercial license under the GI bill.

Ray Christiansen

33

I went to Boeing Airfield for my ground school and took my flying at Lake Union Air Service because I wanted to get my float rating at the same time. There were five college graduates that took their commercial at the same time I did. The thing that really scared me was that they were the ones that asked all the questions that I thought I should be asking, and giving the answers when there was question time. They took the test a couple of days before me and when the results came out only one of the five made it and I knew that I was in trouble. But that made me study harder and I took the test and passed it. After I got my written over with, I took the flight test. I didn't have any problem with that. I never had a problem with flying.

I got my commercial and came back up and fished that summer. That fall I got hired by Bristol Bay Airlines, which was running mail for Pacific Northern Airlines. I flew for them for a couple of years before I quit and went to Anchorage and got hired by Alaska Airlines. I flew for them for about eight months. Then I wanted to get back to Dillingham. I flew for Bristol Bay Airlines four or five years more, and later on we didn't get along too well. I quit. That same afternoon Northern Consolidated asked me to fly for them. I got my twin engine rating and was their relief pilot for a couple of years. Anytime a pilot went on vacation or got sick, that's where I went, whatever airplane they were flying. It was a very good experience for me because I got to know the area. Of course, I knew the Kuskokwim area here because I used to travel it by dog team. Then I was flying out of Fairbanks and I met my wife in McGrath. I took her out visiting friends in McGrath one night and that is when we started courting. I transferred back to Bethel and Tillie and I got to going with each other and then decided to get married. I stayed with Northern Consolidated for almost ten years.

A couple of years before that, I ran for the legislature and made it. I was in the Bethel City Council here and a friend of ours was in the first state legislature, a real nice guy by the name of Jimmy Hoffman, another bush pilot. He ran as a Republican. So a friend suggested I run as a Democrat. I didn't know the difference between a Democrat or a Republican. So I came home and asked Tillie. She told me that Democrats were more liberal than Republicans and go more for the ordinary people and usually Republicans are for big companies and rich people. So, I decided to go for Democrat and I'm glad I did. Tillie said her father voted for Hoover and those were the bad years so he would never vote for a Republican again and he never did.

Later I took advantage of the GI bill again and borrowed money to buy an airplane and start our own air service. We got our certificate and Tillie was the one that actually ran it all the time. She has a lot of experience in bush work. She's very good because she knows all of the villages and she knows how to load airplanes. She did a lot of dispatching and everybody knew her. We had it for about twelve years and then sold it.

During the legislature I was gone a lot and in between times we worked on the native land claims, and I was in Washington, D.C. When we had just become a state, the federal government wanted to enforce all the rules and regulations of spring hunting. They had never enforced these regulations before, but when we became a state they started picking up native people, the guns, sleds and whatever. So, the people asked if I could do something about it. At that time the representative was supposed to do everything. So I talked to the enforcement agents. I knew them because they were pilots like myself. One time I was here and one of the Native people came in here and said, "Ray, you know they just took my dogs and my guns. What was I going to do? And how am I going to feed my family?" The spring hunt in those years was needed for food. Ray Trumbly, the agent in charge of this area, happened to be down here so I told him that he just took this person's livelihood from him. I said, "Can't you just look the other way?" He said he couldn't do that. So I said I would call Senator Gruening. We had telephones then and I called Washington, D.C., and he was in Ketchikan at a Democratic convention. They put him on and he said, "Tell those Fish and Wildlife people that if they don't cut that stuff out, I'll cut their budget." I said, "You go ahead and tell him that." So I gave the phone to Ray who kept saying, "Yes sir, Senator. Yes sir, Senator, but you will have to send a letter or something." I got back on and he said, "Ray, I am going to send you a telegram and you should have it by tomorrow." He sent a telegram, and I made copies of it.

I wanted to get the native land claims passed because when I first came to the legislature, a fellow by the name of Stan McCutcheon came to me and suggested that I get interested. He said that in a few years we would lose our land if we didn't do something because people were moving in and just taking land and the federal government was also taking it for a refuge. So we got together, the AVCP (Alaska Village-Council Presidents), and had our first meeting with about ten people attending. We decided we were going to do something, at least write a bill. Stan McCutcheon was there with Albert Koloa, chief of the Tyonek Indians, and they had just settled their land settlement for seven million dollars. This was a different settlement. They are in with us now but this was their own and it was what gave us or McCutcheon the idea. They said to us, "Ray, we'll loan AVCP $100,000 to start on this. If you guys

Ray Christiansen

35

don't make it you might as well forget it anyway." After we got the bill passed and got our money, we paid it back to them. In other areas I don't know how they started but that is how we started.

AVCP and all these corporations were broke. A lot of times I used my own money and luckily I had my own airplane to bring people in to testify. I brought older people into Anchorage on my own. I talked the BIA (Bureau of Indian Affairs) into getting their transportation into Anchorage and back to testify when the Interior committee came in to have hearings. I am sure I'm not the only one to use out-of-pocket money to go to these places. I had meetings in villages like St. Marys, Hooper Bay, Tununak, Nightmute and Kwigillingok and I took people around and didn't charge them anything because I wanted to get the bill passed. We had meetings in Anchorage altogether, Doyon and Sealaska were there, and others from up north. I think Stan McCutcheon wrote a bill and Senator Bob Bartlett, who was a good friend of Stan's, introduced the bill. It wasn't the bill we wanted, but it was a beginning and it could be amended. We had to work on the amendments. And twenty years ago, in 1971, it passed, the Alaska Native Land Claims Settlement Act (ANCSA). Then we had to have corporations like Calista and Doyon. There were twelve corporations here and the thirteenth one is in Seattle. We didn't want to forget them. They can't get any land but they can at least get 7(i) money.

Section 7(i) of the bill makes a regional corporation share seventy percent of its money that comes from natural resources. We knew that Alaska was so big that some areas wouldn't get any oil, and other areas that had oil would be rich. So part of the money they get, like from the North Slope, comes to us through 7(i). Once we get it, like at Calista, we have to give it out to the various village corporations so everyone will get a little something out of it. I think it is a real good idea. They get good 7(i)s in Anchorage because they have oil there. You can get 7(i) from oil, mineral and timber.

We put the twenty years in so the children who were born that year, 1971, could be shareholders and after that they couldn't. I didn't like that because I would have liked my granddaughter to have land. But that is the way they made it in the conference committee. In those years you couldn't get into the conference committees, they were closed committees. Nowadays you can. We said twenty years so that the kids born back then would be twenty years old at the time when you could sell your stock, and they would know what they were doing. If it was less time, they might say they didn't know, which even now they say - and that if they had been there it would be different. Now it's legal to sell your property if you want to. The settlement has been amended so many times that I really don't know what is in there. That is one of the reasons that we have our AFN (Alaska Federation of Natives) meetings every year.

The first year someone had to set up the corporations. So they just chose five people to run it; there wasn't even an election. Someone had to start right away. Then I got in on the board of Calista and they ran me for president. The president was the chairman. I stayed as chairman for nine years or maybe eleven years, a long time anyway. Finally someone else took over and now I am just a board member. We were losing money for a while but now we have it straightened out - we're holding our own and making a couple of bucks.

Ray Christiansen, "Windy" Reinmuth , Bob Huff, and "Lanky" Rice in front of T-50 Cessna on floats known as the "Bamboo Bomber" 1954
Collection of Ray Christiansen

Ray Christiansen

On looking back, here we had these millions of dollars and we should have invested them to keep going. We made some bad investments. The people up North didn't have to make many investments because they were making so much money. The same way with CIRI, that's Cook Inlet corporation. They had the oil there, too. Actually, we don't have anything out here so far. But when I was flying, I took oil companies around and according to them, there is some oil out there. Another problem we've had is anytime we talk about oil here, conservationists come in and say the people live off the country and if there is an oil spill you won't have that anymore. So the people believe it and now the Exxon oil spill really made it tough. I have been telling my board members that we are going to have to get busy and see if we can talk the people into making some test holes. Actually we have land where we can just say "go ahead," but we don't want to do that because we want the people to make the decision. Anyway, we are doing better.

When they made me president, I was so scared. When you make a decision that is going to affect people for a long time, you just hope that it's a good decision. A lot of people think that the Native Lands Claim Settlement is a bad settlement, but it is the best settlement that any natives have ever had.

I was living here all the time, but I was traveling a lot. I still give Tillie credit for putting up with that because without her we would have no business and I wouldn't have been able to afford to do any of the things that I did.

I loved my flying, but when I quit I didn't even miss it. Now pilots don't even have to go on skis in wintertime. We used to have to go from wheels to skis and in the summertime on floats. The pilots have much better radios now and the airplanes are fixed so they can go instrument anytime. We went on instruments too, but we didn't have the equipment they have now. I made a lot of emergency calls, brought people in just barely living. Now if somebody does that they hit the paper.

Some of the biggest changes have been in the schools. I went to this orphanage school with grades up to the seventh grade. I only went to the sixth. Later on I took correspondence courses to upgrade my education. The schools were so bad when I moved from the children's home to Kwigillingok that the eighth graders were the only ones who could speak English. All the rest of them couldn't speak a word of English. This was about 1935. I don't know how they got to be eighth graders because all of the teaching materials were in English. Those of us who went to the children's home could speak better English than others. They let us speak the Eskimo language as long as we were outdoors. Once we entered the house or school room, it was all English. I used to be able to read and write Yupik until the university screwed it up. They tried to make it international and changed pronunciations. Now I don't know how to read it. Us old timers, people my age, say the same thing. Even the minister here and the bishop said he would have to study these new native writings just like one would study math.

Schools - that was one thing I worked on at the legislature. State schools were all in poor shape. BIA had beautiful schools because they had the money, but they didn't have the school teachers. One little girl came in here one time when we were talking about this. She went to school in Akiachak and said the teacher would ring the bell with his pajamas on and sit there and drink coffee while everybody was coming in. The only time they did anything good was when the superintendent was coming and that's the way it was with a lot of schools. Territorial schools were good, but they were small. After I was in the legislature that was one thing I went after - I wanted the state to take over. After they took over, for a while it wasn't all that good because they were just turning over and the schools were falling apart. Then in those days the school teachers weren't really getting any money. That was the first and only time I ever voted for a pay raise but I wanted them to have a good place to live, better living quarters. Also, if they are out here they should get a few more dollars because it is more expensive. But they make too darn much money now. And that was what I went after, and the airports.

I think being in the legislature was a high point in my life. I got a lot of education in those twelve years. We got airports, schools and all of that. Makes you think that you might have done something.

Ray Christiansen

Rose Palmquist

Wasilla - Her house is surrounded by flowers and her large garden speaks of care and imagination. She greets me and takes me to a large strawberry patch.

I learned early on in social work, during the worst part of the Depression, that when people were forced into new situations they developed new aptitudes and became very competent with their new skills. We talk about the resources in the world and only briefly has anyone ever looked at the tremendous unused resources in humanity. When they have to, people can do things that they never thought they could and nobody else thought they could, and manage to do them quite well. We have some recognition of that because it is a public perception that we elect a president that's equal to the times.

I was born in Morgantown, which is a section of Duluth, Minnesota. It was the steelworker's section where the Mesabi iron ore deposit was hauled to Duluth and converted into steel. I was born on a very stormy January Sunday and my aunt on my father's side came over and said, "Well, hello Rose." And that is how I got named.

When I was about three years old my father bought an eighty-acre tract, sight unseen, with a two-room shack on it at Barnum, Minnesota, and moved his family of five there. It was scratch for a living. My parents borrowed four hundred dollars from the bank, which was a lot of money because at that time you could have bought a good-size house in Seattle for three hundred dollars.

My father didn't milk the cow, he sent my mother out to milk while he lay in one of the two rooms on a bed. My oldest brother who was about ten assisted my mother in the barn. We kids played by ourselves and pretended to milk the cow - we all had garters that held our socks up above our knees and we were milking on the garters, pretending we were milking the cow. My father came along and grabbed a broomstick and started beating us and when it broke he threw it down and went back to bed. That steered me into an attitude, which was very pro-protection of women and children. I turned six the next month and the youngest was a baby girl born the previous July. That fall, just before

Christmas, the barn burned down. There they were with a four hundred dollar debt on the farm, some cows that had not burned up, the chickens and a horse. After the fire, my father took off and we didn't hear from him for a long time.

My mother immediately started selling all the cream from the milk. A neighbor came along with a cow and we had a heifer so fairly soon we had three cows and then we had four. The skim milk was fed to the kids and the pigs and the chickens when it soured because chickens love cottage cheese. We always had cottage cheese, vegetables, scant on the meat and the result was that with all of us working and eating the very finest of foods, we grew up with good bone structure and healthy as horses. In fact, I'm not sure the horses were as healthy as we were.

When my father deserted his family, everybody took a dim view of what kind of family it was. It wasn't that we were the only poor family around, other families didn't have much either. There were a lot of other northern Minnesota families struggling on nonproductive land that were poor, so it wasn't that much of disgrace. It was just that we were kids with only one parent and everyone had

Rose Palmquist

42

*Rose and her family going on a blueberry
picking trip in Minnesota. 1914*
Collection of Rose Palmquist

two parents in those days. The result was
that we were all readers and we were all in
sports. Of course it wasn't too long after-
wards that World War I started and Germans were very suspect anyway. By that
time my mother's brother had joined us to
help out the family and he was eighteen or
nineteen years old. He didn't want to go
over and fight his cousins and the neighbors knew we had relatives in Austria,
Hungary and Germany . We were sort of
outcasts during World War I. I don't know
that we got yellow painted on our doors but
the psychological impact was there.

I didn't know how to speak English
when I first went to school because we
talked in German at home and some of the
English that I had learned was from my
older brother while playing out in the streets of Duluth and was not very acceptable for a little girl. While we were learning to read and write my mother learned
right along with us. She determined that German in the home was not the way
to go in America and we were to talk English. She was all for education.

At first we went to a five- or six-room country school and were in rooms of
one or two classes per teacher. We had a limited library that lasted us until we
went into high school in town. I think I read every single book in that library. I
couldn't take books home because we had chores so I would do my homework
fast and read books in school. The result was by that extra reading I had an
advantage over others who didn't read. Each of us in our turn was the top
student, which we found was no great shakes when we went to the university,
which was a huge school. There, students came from four thousand and six
thousand enrollment schools and we immediately realized where we were in the
scheme of things.

The biggest difficulty I faced in my entire life was getting an education with
no money. Every summer I worked for wealthy families at either Lake

Rose Palmquist

Minnetonka or White Bear Lake, and saved my wages for tuition and a health card, but I couldn't afford books. I worked for my room and board during the school year, so in order to meet the basic study course I had to study at the libraries and check out books whenever I could. Finally I came to the attention of the dean of women, who arranged that I get a student loan from PEO Sisterhood, which I had to pay back after I graduated. I graduated in the four years and having learned that political science was not a good job-getter, I turned to social work. I did well enough in social work that I was hired by the leading agency in the Twin Cities at ninety-five dollars a month, ten dollars a month more than was the going wage in that area.

An opportunity came along later for graduate study working half-time evaluating the social work of the children's bureau. By that time I took on another half-time job as social worker for the Minneapolis Maternity Hospital, which took the low-cost maternity cases, the unwed mother cases and their children. I was to do the placement of adoptive children and the boarding house supervision for those being placed in a boarding home. About the same time the state needed a supervisor in one of the rural counties and they asked me to take it on. The state, at that time, went into the U.S. Federal Transient Program because there were too many transients traveling around the country and becoming a problem wherever they hopped off trains. I was hired as the assistant to the director. We set up camps throughout the state. One was to manage a herd of cattle that was shipped from Montana and western states where there was a terrific drought, into northern Minnesota where we still had green grass. In another camp we had a forestry program. In a third, the question was what to do with the residents of these transient camps. We had a plan to encourage the residents to do various things - some to become shoe repair people, others to write a camp journal and others to become cooks and bakers. We were teaching them these trades so they could later get jobs. For some reason that did not suit some Chicago industrialists who complained bitterly to Washington and got the authorities to shut down the transient bureau in Minnesota, which they did with a heavy hand in 1934. Also in 1934, there was a big Teamsters' strike in Minneapolis, which ended with a success for the strikers. At that time I was an active supporting member of the Office and Professional Workers, which was the only organization that was available for social workers.

Having left my Transient Bureau job, I then applied to other state administrations for employment and in June 1935 I went to work for the State of Washington as a field supervisor located in Yakima. I was evaluating the future of the unemployed and the poor. First they were put on direct relief where they got

Rose Palmquist

44

one dollar and sixty cents per person per week. That was the maximum relief allowance. From that they were referred to WPA employment where they could work a certain number of weeks, and then they had to be off a certain number of weeks.

The migratory workers were treated horribly. Their children were not accepted in any of the schools, they received no local social services, no other local employment and as soon as the work season was over, the county sheriff loaded them into box cars and shipped them out. I decided I wanted to get out of that program because those people certainly had very little future under that system. So I decided I would go into a program that would have a better deal for the working class, and I went back to Minneapolis.

I then worked industriously for the American Federation of Labor (AFL). At that time they were in a competitive conflict with the CIO, a very successful union, which had an entirely different approach - they stayed on their jobs and carried on a non-work program sitting on their work stools. The CIO went after the unorganized whereas the AFL was in essence a crafts union. Nonetheless, I was able to organize the dairy industry and the newspaper industry. When World War II was approaching, the battle between the AFL and the CIO became more heated. I was charged with CIO sympathy, which I did have. This was before the days of having the right to sue when discrimination took place. There was no question that I was a good organizer. But I didn't know how to protect myself.

About the same time, the Japanese attacked Pearl Harbor and we immediately had the declaration of war. So my intended, Mr. Palmquist, and I went to Las Vegas, where we were married and I worked as a bookkeeper for the Carpenters' Union. We migrated from there to Medford, Oregon, where the government was building a military camp and from there we went to Seattle. By that time the shipyards were hiring all kinds of hands. Both Mr. Palmquist and I worked in the shipyards but for different shipbuilding organizations. I worked as an electrician's helper for the duration of the war. After work hours, we participated in Seattle labor union activities.

We had already decided to go to Alaska. My brother was a gold miner in Alaska and every winter said, "Why don't you come up to Alaska where you can always get a job?" He said that during the war there was no rationing up there, the girls got silk stockings and there was never a shortage of booze. My husband went up early with a friend of ours. When it was my turn to come up later that same year, he sent down one hundred and fifty dollars, and said to get the old Model A Ford fixed up, get a trailer, load all the household furniture

Rose Palmquist

45

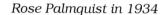
Rose Palmquist in 1934

on the trailer and drive up. In those days on what was still known as the Alcan Highway, you were supposed to have three hundred dollars to get through Canada. I had a twenty month old girl, a five year old boy and a thirteen year old girl. So I went to my mother and said, "I'm going up on the steamship. Will you loan us the money?" She loaned us the money and as we were each allowed three hundred pounds of freight, we were able to take everything we needed and we came up on the steamship *Baranof* that landed at Seward, and we went on up to Anchorage in August of 1947.

In 1949, my husband came home and said the Alaska Railroad was going to hire ten women. They needed more people to check freight in and out. They were not going to hire trucker checkers like they had in the past because they didn't want the women trucking - using those handtrucks. But they would have them check, which is paperwork. A couple of friends of mine were applying at the same time, so we all went down to the Alaska Railroad in Anchorage in May 1949 and got hired. We worked as checkers and we all joined the American Federation of Government Employees (AFGE) and in their next election I was elected vice-president for clerks.

I was the griever and handled the grievances and pursued them up the ladder of management. The railroad was handling grievances pretty much in a "we don't have to do it" stance. I negotiated the agreement that the representative of the union has the right to take company time off to investigate grievances

Rose Palmquist

and to present them to the management. When I would get no response or a negative response from the management, I would write to the Secretary of the Interior - at that time the railroad was under the Secretary of the Interior and not Transportation - and if I got a letter back that was just routine, or no letter at all, I would then write to the President. Or, I might write to our lone representative, Mr. Bartlett, and he would take it up. Pretty soon Washington sent out a representative. During negotiations, I queried that representative as to whether or not he was a member of the working class and that kind of embarrassed him. Management then went to the head of the union and pretty soon Mr. Sanders from the AFGE came out, but he had to back up the employees because after all they are the dues-payers.

So the railroad decided that my labor background connected me with a successful Minneapolis strike which was considered to be anti-war. They thought that they could get by on charging that I was a subversive. At that time, the railroad employees were pursuing a non-payment of overtime pay. So, I went up to Harold Butcher, who was handling the case locally, and in due time it went to the guy in Washington D.C. and they thought that I had a just case. I had a hearing in Seattle on whether or not I was a subversive and then another one in Washington D.C. My expenses were paid and the attorneys represented me for free. It was not the ACLU either, I didn't go through them. In the meantime then, not working for the Alaska Railroad, I settled on a homestead and one of the trainmen (the four big unions in the United States) sent me a message, "Hang in there, Rose, because you should win."

So I hung in there. Finally someone called me up and said, "I am sending you this article in the paper. There is a case exactly like yours over on the East Coast and they just won in a federal court." Eisenhower was President then. I wrote to the Secretary of the Interior and I said, "You just lost a case exactly like mine and I'm here struggling on a homestead with a couple of children still to educate. Why put me to the expense because I will take it to the court and you will lose. So why don't you just settle this?" And he did. He ordered the railroad to reinstate me with full back pay and benefits. Well, they cheated me a little on the benefits, I should have collected six years of vacation time and six years sick leave, but I got paid six years back pay.

When I got the check I showed all the railroaders and even went up to Fairbanks. I wanted the employees to know what was going on and what happens to a union representative when he sticks his or her neck out. And not only that, but the average person that wins in a case like that is quite willing to fade into the woodwork. Not me. I went back to work and immediately became the

Rose Palmquist

union representative again. Nobody challenged my making investigations on union matters or grievances of the employees. I was involved in the beginning development processes on the railroad's health care plan. I worked there until my work was absorbed by IBM machinery in 1961. I could have "bumped" into Fairbanks but I didn't want to move to Fairbanks. I went back to work until 1961 when I was facing a cancer condition and I needed to take care of that. I used my built-up health and seniority time to pay me through the medical care procedure.

I had already been moose hunting in the general Wasilla area and in 1954 I hunted along the railroad tracks in what is now Houston. There was one other family and two military active families that wanted to homestead also so the four families of us decided on filing because it was a good location. We could develop a town at the crossing and it would become a development community. My husband and I had already peacefully gone our separate ways. He did not wish to leave "the sidewalks" of Anchorage, and I wanted to homestead. In the meantime, he had his eye on some other gal, and I had my eye on a guy I thought I might want to marry. As soon as school was ready to let out, we were there with a panel truck, cats and house plants. We picked the kids up at school and moved up. We had moved in a small travel trailer and each of the other homesteaders had bought one too, and we all moved up there in the spring of '55. There was no paving except from the Knik River Old Glenn Highway Bridge into Anchorage.

Then after 1962, when I had recovered from my successful cancer operation, I did odds and ends from then on. I was active in state government policy development, took an interest in everything that happened here in Wasilla and in Anchorage and lived on very little money. Sometimes at the most, seventy-five dollars a month. We raised large gardens. I grew hay for sale for a few years until my daughter went into the 4-H stock raising business and that took up all the hay. We always had all the berries we could use. My son fished so we always had canned fish. Moose, fish and garden produce sustained us.

People think that it is unusual and almost rare for a woman with minor children to go homesteading by herself. But we had already proved up on a homesite at Rabbit Creek and homesteading was not that much harder. Besides I have never lacked for guts; my backbone is stiff.

I lived out at the homestead with the kids from the spring of 1955 until 1971. In 1966 we organized the town of Houston. I was 60 years old at that time. In 1971 I moved to Wasilla.

In fall of 1972 I went to work for the state in Juneau and was there until

Rose Palmquist
48

1976. For two years I worked to put the longevity bonus program into effect. That transition, from working in a union to working for the state, is very easy and normal. If you're working for a union and you think of yourself as being in the labor movement, you are in a political arena representing a labor contingent, and you are thinking in overall terms as to specific terms. Negotiating for a wage increase or against a wage decrease or negotiating with the legislature for senior citizens tax exemptions or the longevity bonus or a comprehensive health plan, to me it's all the same thing. Then I went to work for an outfit called Tri-Trades, which was a combination of the Operating Engineers, the Laborers and the Teamsters.

In 1976 Tri-Trades fell apart and Jesse Carr wanted me to come up to Anchorage and work with the Teamsters, so I did. From January of '76 to September of '81 I worked for the Teamsters as their retiree coordinator. The local union was run by local people and did a lot for its members. Their decisions were made by the members - it was democratic. The local union was not corrupt, but I have never changed my mind about the international.

The thread that runs through my entire life from the later high school years on was to be of some value to the people of this world. At first I thought I could be a Madame Curie, but finding that physics was not one of my talents, I turned to social work and union organizing. Social work is mainly adjusting people to the system. At some time in my social work career I decided to work toward adjusting the system to the people, which is an entirely different approach and that is where I have been ever since.

I don't think any of my efforts were wasted. I certainly helped groups of people better their condition. If that's lasting or not, only history will say. In the political arena you win some, you lose some. In essence, I was more interested in doing a good job at something than earning more money and I believed the State of Alaska had nowhere to go but up. I have told many young people that in Alaska, anyone who applied themselves, used ordinary common sense and didn't drink up their money, would do very well. I still stick to those same words. It is a land of opportunity here. I didn't really begin to worry about personal security until I came to Alaska at the age of forty with three children to support and getting older at a time when it was difficult to get jobs, especially for women. Being an American daughter of a European peasant, I am land conscious. As I have worked I've laid aside bits of grocery money for little plots of ground, thirty-five dollars a month over here, fifty dollars a month for a year or two over there. Inflation set in and I always did very well on land until now when I'm afraid that taxes will eat up all of the profits.

Rose Palmquist

Rose Palmquist celebrating the Fourth of July.
Collection of Rose Palmquist

Rose Palmquist (left) and Ruth Edmondson at a logging operation in 1988.
Collection of Rose Palmquist

Rose Palmquist
50

Yes, I'm in the capitalist system and I don't believe in the capitalist system. I would rather see some type of cooperative government, but I don't have a great deal of optimism about its success. My experience with cooperatives, is that the minute the government begins sponsoring co-ops, they fail. A person owes more to the world than their own maintenance and if they don't produce more than their own maintenance, their real right to exist is lost. I feel that way not only about individuals but also about groups. I have warned senior citizen groups to work toward maintaining economic earnings and independence as long as possible so as not to become a parasitic group upon the rest of society, applying that principle of giving more that you take. When you take more than you give, your reasons for continued existence are weak. My brother said it very simply, "You've got to earn your salt."

I would like to see peace before the end of my life. I think peace is the single most important thing to have happen in this world. The largest amount of the world's resources and gross national products is expended upon war materials; defense, rather than consumer goods. As long as the efforts of humanity are expended on war we will not be gaining in the advancement of cultures.

In a sense I was a woman ahead of my time. I was joining a movement that had already been in existence since the late 1880s when women were fighting for the right to vote, which they got in 1920. I was just entering high school then, so I certainly was impressionable. I've always thought that women should be able to handle their own affairs and not be dependent upon men - who weren't there when they were really needed. I have always been for women to be as economically independent as men.

I am an activist. I would rather make a move and make a mistake than do nothing. The thing that I have found not only with the elderly but with people in general and certainly in the labor movement is that people who are satisfied will not join protests or betterment movements. There has to be some privation or a perceived or real threat to their well being. If workers or people organize, they can improve their lot.

In the way of general observation or advice I would say that change is definitely possible. It has happened at least a couple of times in my life. It takes a lot of willpower, but you can change a lifelong habit that you think is impossible. You can control worrying for instance; you can control happiness over sadness; you can control, to a degree, health over illness. You can make a difference.

Rose Palmquist

51

Edward Edwardson

Barrow - Eddie takes care of his one-month-old great granddaughter. He is holding her, feeding her, and carrying on a steady conversation with her while he talks to me.

For the Eskimo, the whale is a sacred animal. Sometimes a whale will come up to a certain boat and give itself to that boat. It will never go away, just stay right there to be killed. And the Eskimos believe that that whale has the spirit of one of their relatives and it comes to this earth to go back to this family. That's what Grandma used to tell me. The same way with caribou. You go out caribou hunting and there'll be a certain one that comes right up to you. According to Grandma's way of thinking, it's the spirit of one of our people coming back.

My grandmother is the one that taught me everything. Grandma was my home. She would take me out fishing and teach me how to hunt ducks in the summertime. She taught me how to sew our mukluks and fix everything. She used to tell us to be good to everybody, be kind, try not to cheat. And I've kept every word of it.

Once we went out to the river about thirty miles from here. That's when I was around eleven years old and she sent me to Barrow with the dog team to get groceries. I made the round trip back on that day and there was an old man at the fish camp who told me I beat all the men of Barrow. Nobody had ever returned from Barrow in one day and I was only eleven years old.

Dad came from Norway. He was at Kotzebue for awhile and then from Kotzebue him and Dick Hall went to Wainwright. They started a store there. Dick Hall stayed there and Dad went to Barrow. That's where he met my mother and then he had a store at Beechey Point.

My mom and dad were married three miles out in the ocean. Why, I'll never know. And then after that, we went to Eskimo Island, that's where I was born. My mother was Eskimo. From Eskimo Island we came back to Barrow with the dog team and I was not quite a month old. This was in November. And I remember that. The second thing I remember is that we were inside of a snow house.

*Edward Edwardson's mother,
Dora, in 1917*
Collection of Edwardson family

*Edward Edwardson, left, stands
next to his brother*
Collection of Edwardson family

There was a door and Dad was sitting on one side and another man on the other side. I was lying on my tummy looking at the people. All of a sudden the dogs started barking and my dad and the other man took off. They were gone for awhile and when they came back they said they killed a polar bear. I was born in October and this was in November.

After that we moved to Beechey Point where dad had a store. There was a schooner taking the groceries up there. There was Dad, me and Charlie, just the three of us at the house all the time. Dad used to go out and check his traps after we went to sleep at night. The whole coast had people in those days. You could take off a couple or three miles and meet people. They were spread out all the way to Barter Island. And then when Arctic Contractors started, they all came up to Barrow. Nobody lives there on the coast anymore, they all moved to Barrow. When Dad had a stroke, we had to go back to Barrow. This was in

Edward Edwardson
54

1929. I was eleven years old. I stayed with Grandma and I went to school. The first week when I went to school, I was in kindergarten. The next day I was first grade, a week later I was second grade and at the end of the year I was third grade. Then I had one more year of school and then I was a reindeer herder.

I was fourteen years old when I started herding reindeer. They didn't have no reindeer herders at the Brower herd, so they sent me up as apprentice to herd reindeer and I stayed with that herd for eight years. It was fun. We didn't get nothing out of it, but there were no worries. We'd just wake up and watch the reindeer. There was me, my brother Charlie, and Arnold Brower, one of my cousins. We were the reindeer herders.

After I quit the herd, Uncle Sam was ready and he called me. That was in 1942. I was born in 1918. Me and Arnold Brower, we flew Wien to Fairbanks and that's when I got pneumonia at Ladd Field and they turned me loose. Then I worked for the Alaska Road Commission. I was working on the Richardson Highway, going back and forth to Big Delta and Fairbanks. I worked there until 1945, then I went back home to Barrow. Trees don't appeal to me. I got to be up here where it's flat, with icebergs.

Etok, (Edward's father), Fred, Charlie, Henry in front of Cape Smythe Whaling and Trading, 1920's
Photo by Tom Brower

Edward Edwardson

55

Edward Edwardson's granddaughter stands next to his sailboat.
Collection of Edwardson family

Grandma had died. She had left some words to be relayed to me but nobody did. I started working for Arctic Contractors on the DEW line. I was getting about a dollar and twenty-five cents an hour because I was a heavy equipment operator. I learned that from *Popular Mechanics*. When I was a reindeer herder, old man Charlie Brower used to send me *Popular Mechanics*, *Reader's Digest*, *Collier's Magazine*, *Saturday Evening Post* and *National Geographic.* Those were my school books. I graduated from those books and fourth grade. Those books would wear out at the camp and every time the mail come in, there'd be another book from old man Brower.

About eighteen years ago, I saw a cheap sailboat in a magazine and ordered it. I paid eight hundred and some dollars for it. It was a kit. It came up by Wien Air Alaska. Noah built his ark in three hundred years. I built my boat in three years. Every friend I had in Barrow promised me they'd give me a hand in building it, but not even one person showed up. I just took my time and then after it was done, everybody wants to borrow it. We take it down to Dease Inlet and go caribou hunting in the summertime, just to show off. When I was a reindeer herder, Brower's had a thirty-foot boat. It had a mast on it and I used to sail that boat. We'd come in from the cabin way up in the hills and I'd do the sailing. We used to do a lot of sailing in *umiaks* before outboard motors were around.

I worked for North Slope Borough in Barrow until 1975. All my kids are in

Edward Edwardson

Barrow and that makes me happy. I married two times and each time had four kids. I love kids. My family is the most important thing.

I've got solar energy up at my cabin. I hook up a 12-volt battery and I've got 110-volt lights in the house. I can use my electric saw and electric drill with that solar panel.

When we were young, there were no lights outside of the houses and there was only one light bulb in the whole village and that was at the hospital porch. A little 25-watt bulb and that was our guide. It was pitch dark. We used coal to heat the house. They brought it in from Stateside until they started the coal mine at Meade River and then they'd cat-train it down.

One of the older people told me this when I was a child. They don't know where the bowhead whales go in the wintertime. So there's a legend that the whales invited the spirit of one person in Point Hope to go with them to the wintering place. He went with them and he said they have a big gathering place out in the ocean here, and when it was all over and he had been there for a long time, he wanted to go home. But the whales told him, "Don't go as a whale, they'll kill you." So, they sent his spirit back as a seagull so he could mingle around and that's how he came back to his body in Point Hope. Only his spirit had gone out travelling with those whales.

My grandmother told me the story of some people living up in the hills in a tent. One of the old people was ready to die so she called the rest of the people over and said, "I'll show you where we go when we die." Then she pulled up the edge of the tent and said, "Look out." The sun was shining and the grass was green. And this was in the wintertime. She said, "When we die, that is our home, over there." And then she put the tent down and it was dark outside and wintertime.

Try to do the right thing always, that's what Grandma used to tell me. Never make fun of other people because you're hurting yourself even though you don't know it. Every time something gets bad or not running good with me, I just think back and seems like I can hear her voice. She used to say, "Have patience, lots of patience."

The old ways are slowly being forgotten now. They don't try to follow them no more. A lot of times nowadays they forget all about how to go fishing out here in the ocean. You can cut a hole in the ice and get all the fish you want, but they'd rather go over to the store and get pepperoni.

Edward Edwardson

57

Ashley Dickerson

Wasilla - We meet at her homestead. It's quiet, with a presence and dignity that is reflected in its owner.

I was born in Montgomery, Alabama, "Cradle of the Confederacy," according to the big sign that used to be outside the city, which someday I hope to see replaced with a sign that says "Cradle of the Civil Rights Movement."

I went to a private school conducted by New England missionaries, old maids from Boston who pitted their fortunes into a private school for black girls in Montgomery. It only went to the eighth grade. They taught us from the very beginning that we, as little black girls, were as good as anybody. Rosa Parks was one of my classmates, and that's probably what she was remembering when she refused to give her seat to that white man on the bus that night. After that, I went to a public school for one year, at which I learned absolutely nothing new. I got my high school diploma in 1931 and entered Fisk University in Nashville, Tennessee in the fall.

My family was a very comfortable family. My parents were country school teachers, and Father owned a large plantation. My father did something of everything. He was a school teacher, an insurance man, and a farmer, but he was mainly what would be called a gentleman farmer. He had a large crew of hands working for him, and my mother always had help in the house when we were children. We had rows and rows of pecan trees, apple trees, peach trees, every kind of fruit you can think of, and every kind of vegetable. Of course, there were fields and fields of cotton. And on a farm every child has something to do. I can't remember when I didn't have chores to perform. Then the migration came, when all of the blacks started moving into the northern states and there was nobody to work the farm. They followed industry to Chicago, Detroit, and places like that. It was better for them in so many ways. And when the Depression came there was no money. We had to give up our farm, as it was cheaper to live in the city.

I was an avid reader. I always read. I was interested in historic lawyers; I

was interested in Lincoln's life and how starting from practically nothing, he became a lawyer by reading the law. And whenever I hear the expression that women cannot raise a boy, I always think of Lincoln's famous statement, "All I am or hope to be, I owe to my angel mother." That angel mother also happened to have been a stepmother.

But the thing that really inspired me most to become a lawyer was listening to my relatives talk when I was a very small child. I remembered how one of my uncles, Uncle Charlie, had been killed in a plant in Arkansas. He was taking some cherries through an elevator shaft and fell in. And I heard my Uncle Arthur say that he was going to get a lawyer and see to it that my uncle's widow and children would receive compensation up until the time the youngest child

Ashley Dickerson
60

was an adult. And this he accomplished. I thought being a lawyer was the greatest thing in the world, to be able to help people who were destitute like that. Because without that help, my uncle's children and widow would have been objects of charity. Since then, I have had the opportunity to do numerous worker's compensation cases and to be grateful that God enabled me to become an attorney.

I went to law school at Howard University in Washington, D. C. I think that we started off with about six women in my class of which three graduated. I was the first black female admitted to the bar in Alabama. At the time there were three white female lawyers in the whole state and there were two or three black male lawyers, but I became the first black female lawyer.

My dreams were mainly to be an attorney and to help people. That summarizes it. I knew I would have to make a living and I knew that Benjamin Franklin was right when he said, "Keep thy shop and thy shop will keep thee." So I've always kept my shop and my shop has always kept me.

It had always been my dream to go back to Alabama, but I only practiced there three years, because I married and moved to Indianapolis. I loved Indianapolis. I passed the bar, had a good practice and met a lot of wonderful people. I remained there for seven years practicing successfully. But, I came to Alaska for a vacation in 1958, and when I hit the soil and smelled the air, I knew it was something I had been waiting for. I said, "This is where I'm going to spend the rest of my life," and I decided then and there that Alaska would be my home. I wanted to become a member of the bar and to homestead. I was forty-five then and had my forty-sixth birthday in Alaska. I had been practicing law since 1948, and my children, my triplets, were having their nineteenth birthday that same year.

I homesteaded. Growing up in Alabama, the first toilet I went to was an

Ashley Dickerson

outside toilet. But, I'd gotten out of that. After all, I'd been practicing law for ten years, and I'd been used to a bathroom and civilization. But when I decided to homestead, one of the first things that had to be built was an outhouse. And I didn't get my well and indoor plumbing until '62. I loved the land always, and always felt better in the country. I have always felt closer to God in the country. I've never felt lonesome out here.

I had no difficulty getting business. As soon as my doors opened, people were there, and nine-tenths of them were white. As I often say, whites don't trust each other, and blacks don't trust each other either. I remember so well Wendell Kay saying to me, "Mahala, you're going to be admitted to the bar, and you'll take all of my colored clients." Teasing me, of course. And I said, "No, Wendell, you keep them. They will pay you. Let me keep my white ones, and they will pay me." So we kept up that little joke. Every time we went to court from then on, and we practiced opposite each other for about twenty years, Wendell would always be representing a black person, and I would always be representing a white person.

I've had some of every kind of case you can think of, and each time I've done my best to help the person. If that person didn't get everything they were supposed to get, I would say a prayer for the particular judge that night, and for my client, and thank God that I had had the chance to give my best. It's about all I could say, because for so many people, we did get absolute justice. And I proudly state that as I look back over my clientele list, every client that I have represented was financially better off when the case ended than when he came to me. Even though I myself may not have benefited. I would have felt guilty if I had been enriched, and the client had not.

Everybody's going to have some difficulties practicing law and being black and female, I had some. But worrying about what some unfortunate, unhappy bigot said to me or tried to do to me, or thought about me could have put me into an early grave, or a mental institution. But I always tried to say, "Well, unfortunate for him, but I'm me. And I'm going to do what I think I was put here to do. And what I want to do." And that's the way it went. I'm tough. When they made me, they made me to last. And God gave me a skin as thick as a crocodile's hide. So, I've never interpreted it as my having a problem; that person who didn't want to accord me my civil rights has a problem. Those are the persons who are not ready for democracy, who take away the democratic privileges of their fellow men and women.

I think that each of us is a very special creation. And the quicker we learn that, the better off we are, the more successful our lives will be. I remember how

Ashley Dickerson
62

Ashley Dickerson in 1984
Photo by Fran Durner,
Anchorage Daily News

at Montgomery Industrial School - Miss White's School as it was popularly known - Miss White would lecture, particularly on Friday mornings when we had general assembly, and she would take out sweet peas, her hands full and say, "The earth is God's flower garden." She would show us a yellow sweet pea, a blue one, a green one, a purple one. And she would say, "Now do you think God loves any one of these any more than he does any other one? They're all a part of his garden." So that's the way we viewed it. And people who didn't view it that way, people who would call us names as we would pass through their areas on our way to school, we just sort of felt sorry for those people rather than sorry for ourselves.

There's a particular spot in the world for each of us and I pity those who don't find it. Some have no hope; some don't even start looking for it because they feel that they are doomed from the beginning. I believe there's a spot for everybody, but there must be some inspiration - something to enable you to keep up your good self-image. I think children need very positive

Ashley Dickerson

63

encouragement, all the way through, from their parents, their teachers, and whoever else they come in contact with.

The things that are most important to me are the ideals of Christianity, even though it's never been tried, and Democracy, even though it's never been tried. But I think that those two things could save the world. Not that anyone needs to be a Christian, but we should all have an ideal that we strive toward, and a God whom we worship. We have a duty to help each other. That's one thing I love about Alaska. Nature has made us help each other. If you see your neighbor stranded in the snow, you're not going to pass him by. Not if you're a real Alaskan. Nature has made us stick together. Of course, it's changing in many ways because we're getting in so many people from other places where that has not been the philosophy. We are getting too many people who are walking off with the wealth, too many greedy corporations who are taking the wealth out of Alaska. I think we must somehow take charge of some of our resources again.

I still wish the ideals that were set forth in the constitution of the United States and as set forth by the disappearing supreme court, were made into a reality. But right now, things look pretty dismal. The only hope, as I see it, is more mass participation in the government. More voter participation. And each state electing the kind of people who'll give them the kind of laws they want, the kind of laws that will make for a better society. There's very little hope for the country through the supreme court of the United States now. In fact, almost none. There's very little hope through the White House now. Almost none. Those institutions are gone. But they did quite a bit. Without the Warren court, I would still be on the back of the bus.

Every time we start going forward there are forces that will pull us backward. That's the way it goes. We'll probably stand still for a long time until we get a great inspirational guide - somebody like Roosevelt, Jack Kennedy, or Martin Luther King. The masses don't just rise up without somebody leading them, and it looks like we need some more leaders. We don't know what the hope for the future is, but it lies in individuals fighting for liberty and in a new batch of leaders, who must come from somewhere, white ones and black ones.

I think people are fundamentally the same, and it's what they encounter that makes them different. Where there's more space, people have a tendency to act differently because they're not crowded. It's just like if you want vegetables to grow, you separate them. I think people grow bigger inside in Alaska because they have more space.

I've seen Alaska grow more like the South 48, and I've seen people care less

Ashley Dickerson
64

for each other than they used to. I've seen women get fewer rights despite the fact that on paper they are accorded more rights. I've seen them get injustice in court. I've seen some men get injustice, too. I've seen some minorities get injustice. Sometimes there'll be justice and sometimes there'll be partial justice, which is sometimes all we can hope for. So often lawyers get together and decide what they're going to do to the client. I've had so many people come to me and say, "You're my last hope. I know at least you won't be having cocktails with the other lawyer tonight."

When I became a lawyer, I was just doing what I wanted to do. It seems as if I was jet propelled, that there was just nothing else for me to do. It was an obsession, almost. I'm pleased with having been a lawyer, I'm still pleased with being a lawyer. I don't want to forget how to try a case. So I still try at least two or three cases a year, because that's what I love. I like all phases of the law. I love the law, always have, even before I got into it. I longed for it. And once I got it, I was satisfied. All of it isn't interesting, but, when you're an attorney you're close to the people, and no two days are ever alike.

To a certain extent, I've been able to do the things that I was put here to do. I don't think anyone ever does them all. We merely scratch the surface in our lifetime. But if you can convince one or two others who follow you, to take up where you left off, that would make your life successful.

I don't think we ever accomplish all we want to accomplish. If we did that the world would be perfect. My hope, my dream, my aspiration, is a perfect society and I want to do whatever I can toward bringing it about, which means that I do what I can in my little spot. And I've done all I could. I haven't done as much as I would have liked to have done, but I'm still trying. And I'm free. I don't have to do but two things, and that's stay Black and die.   It's an old southern black expression -"I'm gonna do but two things, stay Black and die."

Ashley Dickerson

65

Rita Blumenstein

Palmer - Rita is hard to capture either in a painting, as she moves constantly, or in words, as we communicate more intuitively than verbally.

I was born in a fishing boat in July 1936 and I grew up in Nelson Island. My dad died, so I'm raised by women, and women power. I grew up around women, my grandmother and especially my mother. I grew up different, I guess.

My mother was a hard-working person, but she always used to still have time for me. Mothers today don't have much time for their kids. That's why people are what they are. At that time, you would carry the baby against your body all the time until they're six years old. When the children are six, then they're public. Then the father would take over. Connections between mother and child are most important until they're six. Women should be better educated because they are the first teachers.

My mother never raised her voice when she scolded us. She used her normal voice. She said, "Old people, long ago, used to say that when you tell stories to kids, never raise your voice. That way they listen. When you yell at them, you deafen them and they don't listen anymore. Noise kills that." Stories are part of learning. Learn to listen, to cooperate and to practice. Makes you memorize and train your mind. That's why we didn't have pens. Train your mind, practice your knowledge. If you jot it down, if you don't look at it, you don't remember it. Repeat it to yourself. That's how you computerize it. Use the computer in your brain.

I went to first grade on Nelson Island. Then I went to other schools. I don't like Catholic mission schools. They're too strict and you have to be perfect. I can't understand why people want to be perfect. It means you have to pretend, you know. I didn't like that kind of atmosphere. You learn fast, but it's a different kind of learning.

But the hardest school I went to was how to handle my power. Some people realized that I had powers and what I could do, and they didn't approve. I already knew long ago I could heal. Four years old, I knew. Five years old. I knew because I was born with it. Even before I was born, I knew. My mother and my grandmother were warning me all the time. Never use your hands in anger, become balanced with people, whether they're children or adults. Level with them to their ability. When they're smart, you become smart, when they're slow, you become slow. You just level with them.

When I was eighteen, I start working at the hospital in Bethel. I passed everything for a nurse's aide. I listened to instructions of what I'm supposed to do and calculated in my head. When they'd change it, I'd calculate again and do just the way they told me. I never wrote anything down. I just calculated it upstairs. If I repeated what they said over as they say it, it was recorded.

When I was working in the hospital, girls would make fun of me because I'd never go anywhere. They would go party and when they'd come back they would cry and then laugh. It confused me. Are they happy or sad? I just couldn't figure

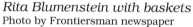

Rita Blumenstein with baskets
Photo by Frontiersman newspaper

Rita Blumenstein
68

out what's going on - what drink does. I started drinking, I tried it, and then I quit. It was dangerous. I see people getting into trouble and I see what happens to the babies.

After that, Dr. Harriet Schirmer hired me. I thought she was either a smart lady or a dumb lady to hire me when there's academic people available that had gone to school for eight years and were registered and everything. I wasn't registered, but I inventoried the medicine without a paper and she knew what I could do, my power of healing. The power of healing is in everybody. It's how it's performed - with kindness, with an open heart.

When we'd do autopsies, of heart attacks or blockage or the brain, and I'd look and I could feel and recognize what I had seen [when the person was alive]. But, I don't know what it is for me - spiritual, physical, mental or emotion.

I was going to be a doctor, a teacher, a nun, a traveler. Now I am everybody. All of them. And I was going to see the world, see what other people do. Now I do more, I'm all of it. More than that! When I travel, I never get homesick, I never get lonesome. I always feel that when I'm far away everybody at home is thinking about me and I'm closer to them. I'm thinking like them. I'm just there because I'm there.

You have to accept all people to become whole. No more that, no more this. You have to be all of them. So it doesn't make any more difference. Like I made an Eskimo Ice Cream Dance. To dance it, you mix it, you pass it, you give it away. I go out in the country, and I say, "This is the Eskimo Ice Cream Dance and I'm gonna dance and this is what the ingredients are. They are berries, fat, water and oil." That's all the ingredients. But when you mix it up, you don't taste any of them. This is what the world is. If you put the white people, Asian people, Indian people, black people and mix them, it doesn't make any more difference. See, you get Eskimo ice cream. Same thing with the drum. I go out all over the world. I bring my drum and beat it and somebody else beats their drum. It looks different but it beats the same. So with your heart, it beats the same. The world's drum is the heart.

I have no idea how I start making baskets. I just don't know. Honest. I just learn it as I go. People make baskets around me, I pick it up - that's the way we learn. When I was fifteen I made a powerful basket. They put it in an international arts show in Juneau. Then after that I got an international award.

I don't count the future. I just take days as they come. Whatever. I don't have any plans. And I like that. I never ever wish, never ever wish I should've done this, I should've done that. Whatever happens happens because it's supposed to be that way. Just accept it. The problem in this world is people don't

Rita Blumenstein

69

accept. They don't accept what happened and they don't accept what will happen. They plan everything and they go by their plans. And they suffer. And they worry that people are not going to accept them. If you accept people, they'll accept you. Just do your pace and don't worry about the time. Rest whenever you feel tense. People push themselves too much. We look at surface, not the depth. People have to change themselves. They have to become honest, pure and open.

When I teach basketry at the college, I explain everything. It's the most tedious, hardest, frustrating project I do. People want to learn from the top. They want to learn everything. And they want to be perfect. I've been doing baskets for years and I have never been perfect yet. I still struggle. And they don't understand that. And most of them don't follow directions. I always tell them, work at your pace. Some of us are going to do better than others even if they've never touched it before. What my mother used to do was she praised me and I want to do more for her. What I did wrong first time, it wasn't perfect, but it was all right. Because I learned from that. Learning from your mistakes. If you look at it, that's a teacher. She also taught me that nobody becomes perfect, you never become perfect. When I think I'm gonna be perfect, I make a mistake. In the world today, you have to be better than somebody. I have to be better than you. But nobody's better than me and I'm not better than you. We all do good. Whatever we do, we all do good. And we all do our best.

Everyone has their gift. Some of us have a gift of mind, some of us have a gift of sharing, some of us a gift of talking, some a gift with their hands, some a gift of looks. Some of us have a gift from inside and shine it out. If we get together then we balance, then we become beautiful inside.

I always tell my students, whatever you learn from this class, I want you to use it as your subsistence. People get mad at me teaching native things to white people. The reason I do is because I don't want it to get lost. Our native people are not doing basket weaving anymore. Basket making is the fastest thing that's going away.

I teach them how to use all the scraps into something. I never let them waste. I try to teach them to preserve, use everything. Long time ago they used everything of an animal, use everything of the wood, the core, the roots, the leaves. I try to explain that it is necessary to respect the spiritual part and also the nature. Because spirit and nature provide us. That's the first thing they teach us, growing up, is to respect animal, vegetable, minerals and people. If you respect all those things, you'll respect God, and those things will always come back to you. That's the real reason I teach, is to teach respect. I feel that when I

Rita Blumenstein

Rita Blumenstein
Photo by Frontiersman newspaper

work with the grass, it talks to me. It's a part of nature and it also becomes beautiful when you make it into a basket.

And I feel the same way with people, like children. If you don't respect them, you walk all over them, you yell at them, and tell them they're no good, then you're surprised that they turn out that way. Just a little respect, a little praise.

My people, I see them as like trees. Some are rotting and their roots are showing or they're not connected to their roots anymore. But when the seeds fall down, new shoots come up and I'm hoping that's going to happen. You see lots of white people alcoholics and nobody notice them. But people notice native alcoholics. They notice us, they worry about us, they make fun of us and they use us. Maybe they'll learn from us.

Balancing is very important. If you pick out all the good grass, the basket is beautiful, but there's nothing there. But if you put in not all the good colors, if you variegate them, then it balances the basket. When you pick grass, you step on it, you use it for tools, sometimes wiping your hands on it. You use it for everything. You use it for putting things on, eating on, or whatever. Everybody uses it and then you make it into a basket, it becomes beautiful.

Just one little blade becomes beautiful. I always feel that people are the same way. Give away a little attention and they can make something out of themselves and then somebody wants them. That's why I teach. I don't teach to become famous. I like the respect part, but famous I don't. But if I become famous, my students will become famous too.

Rita Blumenstein

James A. Sebesta, S.J.

Getting together with Father Sebesta was very difficult . He's constantly on the move. Finally, we arrange a time, and I fly with him from Fairbanks to McGrath and then to St. Marys.

When I was a kid, I think the first clear thought I ever had was that I wanted to fly. We had chickens, and I used to look at those confounded birds and examine their wings, and I tried to build a set for myself. I built them out of some old poster material that my dad had, and some wood. I got up on the garage roof, and as I was getting set to test them, my mother came out on the back porch - and I was just a little kid at the time - she started hollering at me, so I figured I've got to get this show on the road and maybe I can get over the picket fence and get away. But when I jumped off the roof, I was not fully prepared and went straight down and crashed the first time. I broke the wings and got my hide tanned and stern instructions not to try any trick like that again. So I built another set.

One early Saturday morning when everybody was asleep, I dragged those wings up on the top of the neighbor's three-story chicken coop and jumped off. And, boy oh boy, I hit the ground hard, I tell you. I hit it so hard I thought maybe I broke something. So I figured I wasn't going to go any higher, but I still thought I could fly. Then I built a pair of wings for my bicycle. And this time I practiced going as fast as I could, and one Sunday afternoon when there was no traffic I put the wings on the bicycle, and I got on our main street and I got going down that street just as fast as I could. You know how you pull up on the handle bars to go over a curb? Well, I figured that would give me a little lift and head me in the proper direction and I would fly away. As soon as I pulled up, it just all pulled up on me and I came up upside down, going about forty miles per hour, leaving broken wings and paint and skin all over the road. I was about eleven years old.

Then I began to realize that chickens, which couldn't fly, were not a good model and I started bicycling to the small airport just north of town. I wanted to see how airplanes flew. I'd watch the airplanes take off and land. Then one day

Fr. Sebesta adding oil to a plane
Collection of Louis L. Renner, S.J.

somebody offered me a ride. That was great. Then when I was fourteen I got a job at the airport for the summer and I was paid in lessons. That was delightful. The following summer I soloed. It was one of the most thrilling times I've ever had. I can still remember it vividly. I remember thinking, "I'm really flying an airplane all by myself." It was my sixteenth birthday. I look back on those days with a lot of fondness. They were good days because I got in with good people and I learned a lot and I did a lot of things that I would never have had the opportunity of doing if I hadn't gone in that direction. When I was seventeen I got my private license and I worked there at that small airport in Norwich, New York for six years during high school and college.

That's what made me go into physics, this interest in aviation. I was interested in the research aspect of aviation, and not particularly just in flying airplanes that had already been built.

Later when I was studying physics at Tufts University, I became rather seriously interested in a girl. Since she wasn't Catholic, this whole business of religion came up. I was reluctant to just drop what my folks had practiced all their lives even if I did not understand why they did what they did. I began to do some reading, and as a result of some of that began thinking about this person who caught the imagination of these disciples. What was he like? And if he truly was what we believe to be the son of God, he must have known some pretty interesting things. And I thought, "What would I really want to have done at the end of my life that would be important?" I thought maybe research in physics. That would have been a delightful field to have been in. But at the end of that, even if I had made some important discovery, I thought, "Is that what I want?" And I realized that what really did turn me on was to try to make this world a better place to live. That working at something that promotes the well-

James A. Sebesta, S.J.
74

Father Jim Sebesta in 1988
Collection of James Sebesta, S.J.

being of other people - something that is able to fill out their lives in a way that might not have been possible otherwise - maybe making the world a better place to live, would be a better thing to look back on.

And along these lines I thought the present day people who were the equivalent of the disciples were priests. Priesthood seemed out of the question. It didn't fit into my plan. Yet, at the same time, I thought, "What if that is what I'm being invited to and I don't even try to find out?" After some checking it seemed to me the Society of Jesus, or Jesuits as they were popularly called, seemed most suited to my emerging vision and talents. So I wrote a letter to the president of Scranton University, which is a Jesuit University, and I told him that I was interested in knowing more about the Jesuits. At that time they required four years of Latin in a Jesuit high school to even apply. They would never do that today. I suppose it was one way of cutting down the number of applicants that they had to process, because there were a lot in those years. The Jesuit education system was held in much higher esteem then than it is today.

I found, however, that the Maryland Province would accept me with a summer school in Latin rather than a year in a special Latin school. I was accepted into the Maryland Province and went through the spiritual introduction to the Society of Jesus in the Novitiate, through the two years classical studies, and then philosophical studies at Fordham in two, rather than the usual three years, since I had already been through college. Since the Maryland Province required a Masters in some field before going through the teaching phase of the course of studies, I got a Masters in Physics from Fordham University before being assigned to teach physics in Philadelphia.

All the time I was asking to come to Alaska. One of the things that attracted me to the Society was that the Jesuits were in Alaska. But my primary reason for choosing the Jesuits was that they were not just pastors in churches. They ran schools, and did research in areas that I felt I could be active in. They were astronomers, some of the craters on the moon were named after Jesuits, and they were into science and mathematics and research and a lot of other

James A. Sebesta, S.J.

75

things besides just being pastors. That's probably what attracted my attention more than Alaska. I didn't see where I would be all that effective just in church. I thought it would be much more interesting to go to Alaska. There I would be on a different relationship with people than in an established parish situation. When I went to see the Master of Novices for the first time, I said, "You know, Father, I want to go to Alaska." He looked at me horrified, and said, "There, there, brother, just take a good sleep and you'll be all right."

I requested Alaska every year and then finally was assigned to Copper Valley School in Glenallen in 1966. So I taught physics and mathematics and other science courses at Copper Valley. It was a good year. I was, of course, still interested in flying, but Fr. Gallagher, the administrator, didn't quite know how to handle this desire. There were fears such as to liability, expense, an activity not directly connected with the school, which had to be overcome before I was finally given the reluctant nod to fly. Pete Huddleston in Copper Center had a J-3 that he didn't know how to fly himself and he said I could use it if I just maintained it. So for about two dollars an hour I was flying, and I started planning an airstrip.

I photographed the whole area from the air and designed different places where the airstrip should go. Tony Sipary was the maintenance person there and he got excited about the airstrip, too. He showed me how to drive the school's D-6 Cat, and I went out every evening after the boys went to bed and started clearing. That was in April, and in May it was finished.

Flying is something which I have been interested in all my life, and I feel a certain competence in it. I also feel that I have the mental gifts to be able to think in terms that make it not only safe, but enjoyable. It's difficult for me when I run up against restrictions to use this gift, especially when it can be so beneficial.

Fr. Convert, who was then Alaska Jesuit Superior, allowed me to get my Commercial and Instrument ratings before being sent to study theology in Boston. He gave me one hundred dollars to stay current. I interpreted that to mean I should use my ingenuity to do the impossible. A friend sent me the manuals for the instructor's rating. I studied in my spare time, took the written, and passed in good shape. I then invested the one hundred dollars in a one-shot effort to get the instructor's rating. Amazingly I got the rating, and eventually got a job on weekends instructing at an airport near Boston. Part of the money I received from giving flight instruction, I used to get the instrument instructors and multi-engine ratings, and moved into instructing in the Northeastern University professional pilot program.

James A. Sebesta, S.J.

I was sent to Kaltag in 1972 after studying at the University of Alaska in Fairbanks and teaching at Monroe. While in Kaltag, I was also made area director of the Jesuit Volunteer Corps. That took me to all the sites where the volunteers served. Around that time I also flew the deacons to a common site or host village for workshops. In that seven years, I saved the diocese about $385,000 over the alternate means of travel. In those earlier years, I flew Bishop Whelan to many villages. He was very well liked, a deeply spiritual man, and very good to me. The simplicity and goodness of the man was something that I certainly admired.

Being assigned to Kaltag was a positive thing for me, but the initial experience with alcoholism was depressing. It was not something that I had expected in quite the way I had run into it. There was a lot of alcoholism and I felt sometimes very discouraged and wondered what I was accomplishing there. Finally I came to the realization that I had to do something, and not just sit around and complain. I tried a number of things, made mistakes in the process, but learned a great deal. I got very close to the people there, and though I frequently was not able to do anything or solve any problems, people appreciated the attempt, and many times in the long run things did happen that settled problems. What grew was kind of a mutual fondness. Those were good times, even though I argued strongly with some of the people over the terrible problems with alcohol. Yet at the same time I never lost any affection for them. I remember being with the people, especially at night when they get together and tell stories, and they get so wrapped in them it's just like they're experiencing what they're telling all over again. And I look with great fondness on the people down there. Part of that has come from having left behind something of myself, from having tried to give something worthwhile. So I think there's a bond, not only in Kaltag, but in other villages.

This Family Life Program that we're working on now is one of the types of programs that I would like to think will start something that will help people to lead fuller lives. You have to have a certain willingness to understand what people go through. There are certain basic needs and desires that people have everywhere, needs that are beyond culture, and they center around basic love relationships. Husbands and wives are hurt by the same things: a feeling of not being wanted or loved, of not caring, worrying about their children.

What we're trying to do is approach this problem of alcoholism and the dysfunctions that result, through a family program. We call it a Family Life Program. It's not just a treatment program for people with a problem with alcohol. It is a program where all the problems contributing to stress and

James A. Sebesta, S.J.

77

dysfunction within the family are approached - poor self image frequently associated with unemployment, failure to understand the responsibilities of parenthood, abusive behavior, and many more. Hopefully we can help restore healthy family life or introduce it where it has not been experienced. Maybe the outcome will be people feeling good about themselves, being able to communicate with each other in an upbuilding way, and to accept responsibilities and work well together within the family. Children will be given a better start and grow up to be much more productive and happy. Once healthy family life is restored, we will be well on the way to equipping people to deal with the problems that face communities in general. What we hope to do is not only give people the tools for handling the problems they are faced with, but to help them forgive and heal the hurts and resentments that have grown from the dysfunctional behavior of the past.

I realize that we have to be sensitive to local cultural values, but I have experienced in Kaltag and other villages basic common values, such as the need to be loved and appreciated, the need to care for and be cared for, the need to have the offered love returned. Parents love their children and are concerned for their well-being. They are proud and happy when they perform well at school, in village life, in sports, and are disappointed when they get in trouble. Where families have given up on these basic, life-giving parts of family life there is serious trouble. It has happened in many families, especially those plagued by alcohol abuse. Our hope is to help restore these healthy parts of family life so that people can be masters of their own lives and enjoy life again. I certainly don't think I, or any other outsider, will be the one to come in and "fix" everything. But I do hope that we might set up a framework or structure to make it possible to take advantage of this empty school facility and thus enable interested people to take off with the idea. No one, including me, knows how to handle this devastating problem of alcoholism and family dysfunction. But at least I can put my mind to trying to contribute to the solution, rather than sitting back and seeing the people I know and love slowly be destroyed.

I think one of our reasons for existence is to figure out what life is all about. We are here to begin to discover the fullness of God's love for us. We do that through our experience of love. In this life we find ourselves free to do whatever we want. This is absolutely important in understanding the fullness of a love relationship and ultimately our relationship with God. A person can offer love to another, but unless that person is free to refuse to return that love, there is no basis for a genuine relationship. I also recognize that if I am to return God's love of me I must be perfectly free to return it or not. I, also, have to understand

James A. Sebesta, S.J.
78

what that love is, and I come to some understanding of it through my experience with the people around me. The more I understand the very subtle ways human love is expressed, the more I come to appreciate the subtle love God offers to me. This growth in understanding of the fullness of love is the basis for my own understanding of my reason for existence. The more completely I understand, the more genuine my response can be.

During tertianship, I was assigned to something I actually dreaded - hospital chaplaincy. I didn't feel very well suited for hospital work and avoided it, but it turned out to be one of the more valuable experiences of my life. It filled out my own thoughts on the importance of understanding love as the basis for my reason for existence. I was assigned to the cancer ward, where most of the patients were dying. Some people were very frightened of what was happening, and others very much at peace. I gradually came to the realization that, generally, those who had known a genuine loving relationship in their life, were the ones who were most at peace, and the ones who had not were most afraid.

Sometimes people who have lost loved ones or have been faced with really tough times in their lives, try to escape from it with alcohol or some other way. But you have to work through these hard times in order to understand the fullness and richness of human existence and develop in life. It may be very difficult, almost devastating, yet at the same time, it becomes the basis of your experience later on, as you put it into proper perspective. If you don't work through those hard times, you can't grow. When people try to escape the experience through alcoholism, there is no basis for growth and they are less and less able to deal with life.

Kaltag
Otto Geist Collection, University of Alaska Fairbanks Archives

James A. Sebesta, S.J.

Rachel Craig

Kotzebue is a magic place for me - its purple mountains, blue-green sky with the burgundy and straw tundra and the sense of old spirits residing there. While berry picking with me, Rachel says, "My ancestors have probably picked berries in this very spot for hundreds of years...my people..."

When you're growing up, you don't think of what you're learning from the situations in your life. But the way my life has turned out is because I was raised in an Inupiaq speaking family. I've been bilingual as early as I could remember. My mother died when I was five, so her parents raised me here in Kotzebue, and because our house was near the hospital, people from other villages would stay with us and I heard different dialects. My grandmother could speak different dialects like those of the Diomede people, the Shishmaref and the Wales people. My grandfather was more familiar with the North Slope dialects and those around White Mountain and Council. And so, having heard these languages, sub-dialects of the Inupiaq language, I find that wherever I go, I can understand the language. It almost blew my mind the first time I went to Bethel and listened to the Association of Village Presidents at their meeting - I was picking up the gist of their conversations. Their nouns or the connecting words were what threw me off sometimes, but I knew what they were talking about. And this summer I had a Soviet guest and there was just enough similarity between my Inupiaq and her Yupik that we could get by.

After living out in the States for fifteen years, plus being away in school for six years, I was lucky to retain my Inupiaq language skills. My grandmother really tried to educate me in the Eskimo way; to make sure that I would do the right thing when I was with other people. And I knew enough of the culture to ask questions, so every year from when we held our first Elders' Conferences, I worked, pulling information from the elders.

I've always wanted to learn. When I found out about high school, I wanted to go, and it took me two years to talk my grandparents into letting me go. I was at White Mountain School, then they transferred us to Mount Edgecumbe. In January, right after Christmas, I got pneumonia. And what it boiled down to was that the pneumonia was strenuous enough that it opened up my old tuberculosis scars. My mother had died of tuberculosis. So I was hospitalized for years. I went through surgery and I was one of the guinea pigs for the new drugs they were trying. This was the late 40s and early 50s. The only thing you could do for treatment, because there were no drugs, no anything, was to lie flat in bed. But I read a lot. Day in and day out, I read and I read and I read. Eventually the doctors allowed me to study and I finished my high schooling while I was in the hospital. Then I had surgery. I got well and I went home.

Three years later I was back in the hospital again. I must have overworked myself and the tuberculosis was active again. One of the important things I learned while I was in the hospital is that your body responds to how your mind thinks. I made up my mind, after the last surgery turned out to be a failure, and they wouldn't operate on me again. I decided, by golly, I'm going to get out anyway - chemotherapy or whatever it took - a career as a hospital patient was not going to be the sum of my life. I was twenty years old. But, I knew there was more to life than just lying in bed in a hospital waiting for visitors, waiting for doctors reports and just reading. And I, Rachel, wanted to experience things like marriage, children and a job.

But I don't think I was any different from any young people. When you don't really understand life and the purpose of life, you tend to feel sorry for yourself. And I did. I felt sorry for myself and that's really a destructive feeling. So when your mind makes up its mind that it's going to do something, your body responds and things began to happen and I did get well. When I got out of the hospital, I went to school in Seattle and that was really good for me. I completed the two-year secretarial course in one year because my English language skills were so good from reading so many books while I was hospitalized. My class-mates were blacks, chicanos, orientals and whites. Every kind of group. And I found out that if I did my homework, I was just as smart as the rest of them. Heck, here I was Eskimo and my grades were just as good as theirs.

In the meantime, I met this wonderful guy and he changed my plans and my life. We've been married 31 years. I got married and we became parents of a son. And by the time he was a year old we wanted to start taking him to church so he could get some spiritual upbringing. We were introduced to the Church of Jesus Christ of Latter-day Saints. That changed my life. My spiritual quest and my study of scripture and my dreams began to come together. I began to be proud and grateful to be born to this particular Eskimo family, to learn of our history and to take pride in being who I was. I didn't have a church-cultural conflict anymore. Everything came together for me then. I could worship God and still maintain my Inupiaq identity.

Rachel Craig
82

When the Alaska Native Lands Claims Settlement Act passed, there were so few natives that were trained at anything that after a meeting in Seattle, John Schaeffer asked if I would consider coming back to Alaska to work with him. It seemed like a good idea to me. I was happily living in Auburn, Washington, where we had a three-bedroom home on two acres. Life was wonderful but sort of lonely. People out there don't go out of their way trying to know you. Here, you know, everybody knows everybody. I think my husband and our son reluctantly came up here but, I knew we needed all the help we could get and I wanted to do my share. My language skills, even then, were valuable. I could go on radio and talk with our shareholders about what the corporation was doing and do local, world and NANA news in both languages.

And then my husband brought us back to the States. But I had a summer job to do a survey in the region where our ancient cemetery sites and historical places were. And the job became much bigger than I anticipated because the people out there were just so eager to tell us what they knew. It was then that we realized that there was still a large body of oral history that none of our generation knew. Eventually we were funded from the Alaska Bicentennial Commission to have our first elders' conference. And then we had five or six subsequent ones. We worked at retrieving our oral history and that really was magic in a way. I learned so much. A lot of things that I knew inside of me were verbalized. And what's amazing is that the things that our elders in NANA region were talking about were similar to what the North Slope people talked about and there's lots of distance between them in mileage. As I worked with those people too, I found out that a lot of them have words in Kobuk; that the Kobuk people and Noatak people, following animal migration routes and food sources, ended up on the North Slope. So, the more you know, the better understanding you get of why things are the way they are.

I got so much information that I had to hire six other people to help translate all the material from eleven villages. Actually that work eventually became the basis of our Inupiat Ilitqusiat spirit movement. Down the line we realized how many social problems we had - a lot of suicides - and we started trying to understand our problems and how to correct them. And the only thing we could turn to was our traditional oral history, the wisdom of the elders, the wisdom of the centuries. So we, the spirit committee from Maniilaq, from NANA, and from the school district, came up with our Inupiaq values and they have become the basis of the philosophy of this area. We traveled to the villages to see if the elders would approve our lists and every one of them did, saying that these were the things our forefathers talked about. I've been busy with that area ever since.

Rachel Craig

83

Evelyn Henry is stringing net. In the background seal meat is drying on rack. Some of it is for dogs, some for people. Kotzebue - Circa 1950
Collection of Nancy Baker

Kayak races. The kayak framework is made of wood and bone, lashed with rawhide and covered with ooguruk skin. Kotzebue - Summer of 1950.
Collection of Nancy Baker

When I was director of the Inupiaq Materials Development Center from 1980 to 1983, we always had to have a certified teacher working with us whether they knew the culture or not. I always felt within myself that I was intelligent enough that I could do college and I could be that certified teacher. We met a lot of college graduates around here and maybe in technical areas they were smarter, but in overall intelligence they didn't seem any wiser than we were. Finally I had my chance one year. My husband wanted to be in the Seattle area, because his dad was very ill. But I knew the only way I could take stateside living was to keep my mind busy. I always wanted to go to college anyway, so I enrolled at the University of Puget Sound for my first year. I thought that was really good because their expectations were high.

I didn't expect it to be easy when I went back to school, and it wasn't. I took Spanish for two semesters and I never worked so hard at anything in my life. I took a foreign language because we would have to teach our Inupiaq kids the Inupiaq language and I wanted to know how much energy it took to learn another language.

It just seemed I was guided into the job. Other native people in the state saw the beauty of it because they were all looking for the same thing and so everywhere in Alaska, it's sort of like a native/cultural renaissance. Now our respected elders are involved in it. We have Elders' Councils in the village, Regional Elders' Council in the region. They make decisions and our executive people carry them out. Nothing is perfect yet. We're still working on how we might strengthen our culture and our sense of identity.

Rachel Craig

84

I know there's a lot of people who know a lot more about the culture than I do and who speak Inupiaq a lot better than I do. But very few of them come forth to do that work. I'm just grateful to be doing what I'm doing. When I was in college I studied people who had been impacted by Europeans and were able to successfully maintain their culture and their identity. And from my study, it appears that those people consciously chose leaders that were strong supporters and practicers of their own native culture. In that way they would make sure that the cultures were maintained, and that they had control of the comings and goings of the outsiders. They took what was necessary to make life easier for them, but they shut doors on things they felt were detrimental to their culture.

We have to learn how to make our decisions and chart our destiny as other people do. We've never had that before; BIA always made our decisions for us. But now we're beginning to do that and I think our children who are raised in that kind of environment will have an even stronger insight, coupled with formal education either through technical schools or post-secondary schools, colleges and universities. And we would like to make Inupiaq studies really strong, teach them to speak Inupiaq and know their own traditional culture. Because if they feel the strength of the Inupiaq culture within themselves, then they'll be equal to learning anything. I think that's part of what gave me my confidence. I think college is a two-way thing, you learn a lot, but you also give a lot. You're put in classes where sometimes you don't agree with the professor. And sometimes I had to speak out because I felt I owed it to the students to be hearing the right things, not slanted things by professors with no knowledge of how we live in the village.

I think the most important thing in my life is that I have found a spiritual home, that influences me. That is as much a part of my day-to-day life as eating and breathing. It's given me a sense of responsibility to other people. And I think it's true that in life, the more you give to other people, the more comes back to you. You know, you don't expect it to work out that way, but it does.

In previous BIA schools, the Inupiaq language was discouraged and so we almost lost it. But if we do what the elders say we should, and start immersion classes in the first three grades, then we could start really hoping that the language will be safe. If we don't do that, we might as well kiss it goodbye. There are people who are working on how to effect an immersion school. It might be an after-school activity and if it is, we can make it work quicker. Then parents could also be involved because they also need to know Inupiaq.

Rachel Craig

Then they can talk with their kids and learn together. I would like to see that happen.

And I would like to see our families strengthened, our young people more responsible for their education, learning to work and earn, and taking responsibility for their actions and not relying so much on the grandparents for the care of their children. There are things they could be learning in college or in technical schools so they can have jobs in their villages. Like if they learn to be teachers, they have a job at home with their summers off. I would like to see that happening more. Then with learning, they could make a better life for themselves and their family. But even before that, I think the important thing is to gain an understanding of the spiritual life and make it an important part of their lives. Then everything else falls in. It's the same as our Inupiaq values. If you look after the spiritual realm, the rest of the Inupiaq values just fall right in. You don't have to really work at them. Those three strands: education, spirituality and cultural knowledge with understanding intertwined. Those are the three things I would wish for every family in this region. It's universal.

In my growing up years, in the 40s, I felt like we were everybody's children. No matter who we were or which neighborhood we were in, the grown-ups always corrected us, they'd tell us right then and there. They don't do that anymore. There's this thing about civil rights or the rights of people to do or to be what they're going to be, and let so-and-so take care of his own kids. Well, you have to take care of everybody's kids, if you want your kids taken care of the same way. There's no isolation in raising children. I think all of us need to take more responsibility for the actions of our youth, no matter whose kids.

Every youth needs to know who they are. My mother died when I was five, and when I was growing up I didn't know who my father was. I was born out of wedlock and while growing up, I think I knew that in the back of my mind. But you hate to admit it because there's a certain shame and embarrassment that goes with a situation like that. And it took me many years to come to terms with myself. And I felt sorry for myself a lot of times.

When I was a teenager, I really needed to know who the other half of me was. Evidently my mother told her girlfriend before she died who my dad was and so I wrote to her and found out. Then I wrote to my dad and asked him and I started to realize the other side of my family. Not that I was proud of him. There's a lot of anger you have to work through. There's a lot of embarrassment you have to overcome because every child expects their parents to be perfect. Fortunately I had grandparents who were perfect models for me. But my own parents, I couldn't talk about them. I couldn't talk about that situation until

Rachel Craig
86

Rachel Craig in Kotzebue
Collection of the Craig family

after my dad died, because I didn't want to embarrass him. But because there are so many young people in my situation, I decided I would go public and start talking in Elders' Conferences. And I've had some young people come to me, thanking me for making that illegitimacy public because they went through the same thing. I'm talking about it now just to help the other young people work through those strong emotions that they have to go through. Once they gain an understanding of who they are, life will become much easier for them. In the outside world I always felt capable of learning. It's just how much effort you want to put into what you really want. It's coming to terms with myself that was the hard part.

I haven't lived long enough to accomplish anything. I don't think life has a single focus. It's a complex of different things that come to you, the outside influences - money, politics, social standing and religion. I just hope that the young people will feel that if Rachel Craig can do it, they can do it, whether it's coming to terms with yourself and who you are and your identity, or going to college at whatever age. And then working and doing the best you can. I've worked with the elders for so long, now I'm in the Elders' Council myself. All of a sudden, the decisions I make carry more weight. I have to be careful, think my way through and speak to issues in the way that is right and good.

And I worry about our young ladies. They're so eager for love that first thing you know, these beautiful, capable ladies who could have a great future and make great contributions, all of a sudden are pregnant and they're still single. And I know their dreams are still in there, but they can't get out of their responsibility now, because a child is your responsibility. I wish somehow we could teach them that they are loved, that they don't have to submit to sexuality so early, because that's not the total of love. It's a wonderful way to express yourself with the one you love, but wait until they are married so that there's somebody else to help them raise those children, to help support them. They don't realize the heavy psychological burden that they are placing on these children, who will have to work out their anger, work out their shame, work out their embarrassment, the same as I had to. And while you're working through those things, you can accomplish something, but unless you come to a realiza-tion of your identity, and forgiveness, and understanding, then too much of your

Rachel Craig

87

attention and emotions are wrapped up in those hard feelings. And it's difficult to teach them to respect men, when the men have not taken the responsibility to be the legal father.

I think we really need to teach our children to love their forefathers so that as the current culture bearers we can take pride in our own contribution to the long line of ancestors that we've had before us. And today we are the current generation molding the future of our young native people.

It all starts in the family. If we as parents would just work with our children and teach them. If we just live that way, that will become the normal way to live. It shouldn't have to be something that we have to teach. It should be our way of life and they learn right along with it. That's what our grandparents did. I knew the seasonal rhythm not because they taught me, but because they lived that way. We always went to our seal hunting camp in the spring, before the ice broke up, and got out our black meat and seal oil and everything was fresh: fresh ducks, wild eggs, greens, blackberries and cranberries that overwintered. Everything fresh. No wonder we were healthy. And then we'd go to our summer camp where we'd fish and pick berries. And then they'd bring us back to Kotzebue, not because they wanted to come back here, but because we had to go to school. I think it all starts in the home. What you're focusing on, that's what the kids will learn.

I think we have to love our children enough to teach them everything. Not only how to behave at home, but how to behave out in the larger society, and to respect other people and other people's property. Teach them to be truthful; because once people find out you're a liar, no matter what you say after that, they won't believe you. We have to love our children enough to teach them all of these things. I was fortunate that my grandparents loved me. My grandmother taught me a lot of things that her father taught her. My grandfather talked to me about a lot of things. He wanted me to know who my relatives were in different villages and I wished I'd had a tape recorder at the time but I didn't. And I'm not good at remembering Inupiaq names. They came from humble families, like everybody else, but he was a good hunter and he became a carpenter and so he provided well the essentials of life. But even if you don't remember everything word for word, you remember the feeling of concern and love, that protectiveness and the expectations they had of you so they could be proud of

Rachel Craig

Mary Johnson is boiling her muktuk in water. She will boil it for an hour and then let the water drain off. It is then ready to eat or store. Kotzebue - Circa 1950
Collection of Nancy Baker

you. I don't remember some of what they told me word for word, but I remember the feelings.

I think people need not be shy of feeling love for one another. That's a very strong emotion. And when someone's given you a kind word, those kind words carry you far, and inspire you to do more even than you thought you were capable of. People need to love each other. Our children need to love their grandparents, their forefathers. Our young parents need to love their children, not in the sense that they give things to them, but to discipline them and teach them to behave themselves so they won't be embarrassed when they're grown up. They will have learned how to behave themselves before they leave home.

Everybody has to get replenished. You give and give and give and there comes a time when you need to take and take and take and refill. One of my great fortunes is my husband. He's always been supportive. He doesn't like to be in the forefront, he'd rather be in the background than be this white guy that's trying to cash in on native things. It's like he's given me a safe haven.

Sometimes when I have to make an important decision I have to fast, maybe a day, maybe two days and I pray every time I feel hungry. And I fast and I pray. And then I begin to see what I must do. Then when I've gotten my direction, then I go about with renewed energy and do my work. Sometimes you can't go to your boss, you can't go to your husband, you can't go anywhere else. The decision is there and you don't really know which way to go. There are situations in life that drive you to that.

I love to laugh, I love to sing, I love to dance. I can be serious just so long. It drags you down after a while. I love to schottish and polka and waltz and all those things just as much as I love to Eskimo dance. I love being with people, especially those who know my background and can joke and tease and I'll give the same right back to them. Because that's a sign that they like you. I'm just grateful to be alive today, to have my family and to have a job. And to make whatever contribution comes my way.

Rachel Craig

89

Harriet Jackson Schirmer

Wrangell - She takes me on a tour of Wrangell and tells me, "There's this wonder-ful collection of petroglyphs here, and I always think of it as the original artist's colony."

I grew up in the very fortunate place of Oyster Bay, New York, Theodore Roosevelt's home. We were there because my father was assistant to Dr. Derby, Theodore Roosevelt's son-in-law, who was a surgeon. We grew up in the shadows of the Theodore Roosevelt family and in lots of hand-me-down Roosevelt clothes. It was a good, inspiring influence and I'm sure it has had a lot of effect on my life.

My mother was a pediatrician and when I was about two, we moved into a big house that had room for more offices and more family. It was in an area where people were very wealthy and very poor and they both mixed in the waiting room which was the main hall of our house. The opera singer's kids and the Speedwell kids - Speedwell cared for children from the inner city living lives of desperation of some sort - were likely to be in the waiting room at the same time and they were treated equally well.

I spent my summers sailing with the well-to-do and the rest of the year playing with the kids in town. It was an interesting and unusual chance to see the extremes of wealth and recognize that the kids who went off to fancy schools and whose families had lots of money weren't any better or any happier.

My father told me at an early age that maybe when you're young, what's on the outside is important, but after awhile, it's really what's on the inside of people that's important. And I needed to know that. He taught me so much - love of medicine, love of people. He gave me the impression I could do anything I wanted to.

And somewhere along the line he told me that he found general practice more satisfying than surgery because following people over a long period of time was what gave him the most satisfaction.

That made a big dent in my brain. And even before I went to medical school I saw galloping specialization, with obstetricians looking down their noses at

90

family practice/general practice doctors who caught a baby. These doctors were chastised by surgeons if they opened a boil, and they were looked at askance by pediatricians if they saw anyone under fifteen. It just did not bode well for the next umpteen years in that part of the country if you wanted to do family practice. I didn't want to go South. I knew I'd open my mouth too soon in the wrong place and be in trouble. I'd grown up too close to my black friends. I thought I'd like to try Alaska. So before I went to medical school that was my aim.

I went to college in Michigan and to New York University Medical School. I was nineteen when I finished college and twenty-three when I finished medical school. Then I took a two-year internship and a two-year general practice residency in Denver, telling people all along that I wanted to go to Alaska. So they taught me all sorts of extra surgery. I was at the Denver General Hospital. The big tuberculosis research center was there at the National Jewish Center for Immunology and Respiratory Medicine, and I would go over to all their conferences and it was really good preparation. I knew that I needed to be trained better than average because I was going to be off by myself.

I applied through the Alaska Native Service which wanted me to go to Barrow. Then I got a letter saying we need you more in Bethel. After having considered Barrow for two weeks, Bethel looked absolutely wonderful, almost tropical. I got to Bethel in 1954.

As I went through Juneau, Dr. Hinson, the Medical Director for the area, said, "There's more up there than any one person can do. It's more important for you to be alive and working than it is to try and do everything. I don't want you to kill yourself." A most reassuring thing to say and quite an insight.

John Ferger, the doctor I was replacing, passed the whole place over to me in three days. We were running seventy-five people a day through the outpatient department with interpreters. We had close to fifty patients in the hospital. And in less than a month we had to put in the annual requisition for medicine, sheets, food, chlorination supplies, oil, everything that you need for a hospital. They had no records to work from because they had been in a ten-bed quonset until three months before I got there. Some of the stuff in the pharmacy had been brought up there in the 1920s. There was stuff that I'd read about in my grandfather's notes.

Lots of times I thanked God that I had what I needed. On the way to Bethel they had sent me to see Milo Fritz in Anchorage, and he told me what he thought we should be doing about ears and tonsils. And they had sent me to Joe Shelton's office to learn to do refractions which was a godsend.

When I got out to Bethel I had to use all my surgical skills. When I first got there I was the only doctor and there were only three planes a week, unpressurized, and it was a four hour air trip into Anchorage. To get to the airport from the hospital, you put the patient, who was on a stretcher, in the back of a four-wheel drive pickup and went down to the river bank. You then transferred the patient to a boat, went a mile and a half across the river, which was often rough, took the stretcher out of the boat, and put it into another pickup that went to the airport. And then, if the plane got out, you took the patient to Anchorage.

There were lots of people who were too sick to move. So if somebody came in with a ruptured appendix or needing a Caesarian section, you did it. You didn't consider transporting them. You took care of them. But every so often I'd remember what Dr. Hinson said. And I always felt that if I hadn't been there, whoever else was would probably have been not as well trained as I was. You can't do everything right. But you do what you can. Things happen that scar you and affect your life. I think also having survived those problems matures you, makes you a little more considerate of other people, a little more forgiving.

One winter I made a trip to Nightmute and Tanunak. We stopped at Chefornak. The people there wanted me to stay over and offered to take me to Nightmute the next day. So the next day, after seeing whoever wanted to be seen, the men took me and the x-ray machine to Nightmute. Travelling with five teams, averaging eleven dogs each, running beside each other across the trackless, wind-swept tundra - so featureless that the men all carried compasses on their sleds - was a great experience.

Times have changed so much that it's hard for people to realize how things were forty years ago. When I got there the only people they were sending to the TB sans [tuberculosis sanatoriums] were the people with minimal tuberculosis. If you had a cavity or you had advanced disease, they didn't send you to the san. This was a "tough love" decision on the part of the health department because they knew that if they took their worst cases out, they would never come back, and the people would think that if you went to the san you were just going there to die. So they took people who had a good chance of getting better, who could come home. But in the meantime, the people who were most contagious were home. There were only three public health nurses for that whole big area. They had done a wonderful job teaching people about contagious disease. But when you have families of eight living in sixteen feet by sixteen feet houses it's very hard to prevent cross-contamination. And when you add to that questionable food supplies and cold temperatures that force you to keep places closed up tight, the communication of disease is very hard to prevent.

Harriet Jackson Schirmer

Rita (left) and Harriet (right) celebrating the fourth of July in Kwethluk, 1958.
Collection of Rita Blumenstein

So when the antibiotics came, it revolutionized things in many ways. All the TB sans in the states emptied out and the people even in the villages were beginning to get better at home. Within three years, it went from having a three year waiting period where you couldn't get on the list unless you only had minimal disease, to being diagnosed one day and going home the next. It was a revolution.

After three years as medical officer in charge of the Bethel hospital, I felt I was caught between the Public Health Service, which was trying to make the Bethel hospital like the Staten Island Seamen's Clinic, and the people of Bethel and what they wanted and what they needed. I wanted to get out of there, but I liked the country and liked the people and had in my mind that if I could save enough money, I would come back and be in private practice. So I took a two-year job as director of the McGrath Project which was funded through the Alaska Department of Health, to see if health education could change the incidence of deafness due to chronic ear infections and blindness due to chronic eye infections.

When I went back to Bethel, I rented a house from the Moravian Mission and opened private practice. It was a big house by local standards. We had a kitchen, dining room, living room and waiting room, and a little ante room to the examining room that was the business office. The examining room had an x-ray table and an examining table. Another room was the lying-in room. That's where people came who were in labor or stayed until they wanted to go home after they'd had their baby. Upstairs there were two bedrooms.

I was in competition with the government and at least one-half or two-thirds of my patients were Natives. The non-natives had to come to me, because they couldn't go to the government doctors, but most of them didn't mind. My ability to do refractions made private practice possible. People from out of town would come in and I would examine their eyes and refract, and get them glasses and a variety of frames and they didn't have to wait for two months for an appointment at the hospital. Being able to do the refractions made the difference between whether I could eat or not. I delivered about forty babies a year in the facility. If people had complications that I didn't think I could handle, they could be admitted to the hospital but I couldn't take care of them there. Nowadays regulations have changed and a private physician can take care of patients in the Bethel Public Health Hospital.

I heard about Don before I met him. He was the new White Alice supervisor and he was different. He picked up the boys along the street and took them to Sunday School. Other White Alice people tended to spend their time at the bar at the Air Force Base. I met him at friends' and he later came over because he needed an x-ray of his toe. He invited me to go flying. It seems that he wanted to make sure that anybody he was going to do anything with liked flying because there was no sense in getting serious about anybody who didn't. He was thirty-three or thirty-four and I was thirty-four or thirty-five. We got engaged in about a month and a half and got married in October '61.

In 1965, we went to western New York when my mother decided to retire. There was an acute shortage of physicians in the area and it's twenty-five miles from the nearest hospital so we decided I would practice so my mother would not have to. We were there for about five years then Don decided we were coming back.

Wrangell is a really nice place if you choose your friends and your work is satisfying. And when the sun comes out it's absolutely gorgeous. I think one of the nice things about practicing in a small town is not only do you get to follow people over a period of time, but you get to appreciate the good things about people who impress you at first as bums, and you learn that people who look like angels to start with, are human. And you learn to care for them all even though you may not care for a lot of things that they do.

We got a boat because of numerous things. I often saw people coming in for things they shouldn't come in for, chartering airplanes and spending two hundred and fifty dollars for something they could have taken care of themselves, and not coming in for a lot of things that they really should be seen about. It seemed more sensible for the physician to go to the patient than the patient come in to the physician.

So, we started looking for a boat we could put an office on. It was not easy and we finally sold our sailboat and bought the Enchantress. We put in

Harriet Jackson Schirmer

95

an x-ray machine and Don built an examining room and desk, bookshelves and drawers. We could do more on the Enchantress than I could do in my office. We could take blood samples and do minor surgery. It was well set up for ambulatory medicine. So for ten years we tried to get out regularly to about ten or twelve places. We didn't always make it on schedule, but we went to places like Point Baker, Port Protection, Wooden Wheel Cove, Labouchere Bay, Edna Bay, Port Alexander, Whale Pass, Coffman Cove and Bradfield, and sometimes we went to Thorne Bay and Meyer's Chuck and one year we went to Craig. It took about eight days. The nice thing about it was we travelled every morning and in the afternoons we'd see the women and children before the men got home from work and in the evenings we'd see the men.

We picked up at least two early cancers, people that probably would not have gone in for check ups. Both of them are still alive. And we were able to save a lot of people a lot of anxiety and travel problems. I did the school physicals for the people out at the little schools in the logging camps.

Lots of people out there don't know who to go see or how to get an appointment with somebody when they go to town. So I would talk it over with them and try to help. When I came back to town I would call the appropriate consultant and get word back to them about their appointment.

The boat was a mutually good thing. We liked it and the people in the villages liked it. The kids would run down and Don would play games with them or play the accordion. It was fun.

One of the things that's been interesting here has been improving emergency medical facilities for the town and the island communities. When we first got here, if something happened after five in the afternoon, there was no way to get in touch with anybody in town. They had to wait or make a five-hour boat trip. Now there's twenty-four hour availability and people who train as EMTs. In town, our EMTs have come a long way and are doing things that years ago nobody would ever think of letting a non-professional do.

We need to allow people who are trained to do something, do it, if that's a need in the community, and not worry as much about licenses and credentials as about ability. In medicine we have to keep in mind that the patient is the most important person involved; what you do should be for the best interest of the patient. So you have to protect the patient from people doing things they don't know how to do, but get the care as close as possible to the place where they live. And that's one of the biggest problems with the high-tech business. It's so expensive that the best care gets further and further away.

I feel much more hopeful for the alcoholic than I used to. I see lots more

Harriet on the "Enchantress" 1981
Collection of the Schirmer family

people who have gotten away from drinking and who are willing to help others about it. I really think the same will happen with drugs. And we now have a system where it's beginning to be possible to do something for the abused kids, wives, elderly. We don't know how to do it well yet, but there's a concern and I think that the rest will come.

Alaska gives you an opportunity to see that your life makes a difference. When I was in western New York I felt that I was on a treadmill, running at full speed and falling a little behind all the time. In Bethel and Wrangell you have the feeling that you can make a difference in many ways and to me that's important. Doing your best wherever you are is important.

The best and most important things in my life are family, meeting my husband and having my son, and faith. Having the opportunity to be a physician is important, but I could have survived doing something else and I couldn't have survived without the others.

Now, I find myself a little bit out of tune with all the high-tech medical things and I really think that peoples' spirits need more help these days than their bodies. And that's one of the reasons I want to spend some of these coming years helping people with their spirits. I see that as a higher calling perhaps. The purpose of life is probably to pay attention to God's wishes for us and to care for our neighbors. Even if you ended up at death with nothing happening or coming back as a cow, it would have made life much better to have believed through this life because it gives a foundation on which to build your decision making.

Harriet Jackson Schirmer

97

Donald K. Schirmer

Wrangell - He sits at his computer practicing simulated landings and take-offs. He still loves to fly, even this way.

I guess it all started back in Washington, about six miles out of Newport. We were a very poor family and we were on welfare just to stay alive.

It seemed like my mother and I were at home alone all the time because my dad and older brothers were away apple picking or whatever. There was no close neighbor and no kids to play with so I essentially grew up alone. Once in a while if someone came by and left a magazine, it gave me dream material. I'd see a beautiful scene and these things started planting little seeds in my mind that I someday wanted to travel. I felt that there was no hope for me ever travelling. But we had an old pump organ and I'd sit there and "drive" by the hour. The two pedals on the floor were my clutch and brake and a pot cover was the steering wheel. The stops would be the choke and the throttle.

My parents were Christian people and gave me a very solid belief that I appreciated many times later on. My mom was the type that would not go to bed until she had actually knelt down and prayed. My dad was in very ill health and I don't ever remember him standing up straight and tall; he was always bent over.

He was born in Basel, Switzerland. My mother was Chippewa Indian and was born in Whitefish Point, Michigan.

I'd pray all the time that God would just let me travel, anywhere, and let me play the organ, and God has answered both prayers quite well. I've been around the world about seven times.

My dad died in 1939. I was eleven years old. I lived for a year with my aunt who was a missionary to the Hopi Indians in Farmington, New Mexico, and then they put me on the Greyhound Bus to go all the way up to Michigan where my mom and my sister were.

As years went by I had a problem. I couldn't concentrate. I didn't feel I was stupid, I just couldn't stop daydreaming. So in 1943, I was sixteen years old and

The King's private Convair 340. King Saud (white head dress, directly under prop) Crown Prince Faisel (standing at King Saud's left) Jedda, Saudi Arabia in 1955.
Collection of Don Schirmer

we were right in the middle of World War II, and I found out that you could actually get on one of the ships in the Great Lakes with your parents' consent. So that's exactly what I did. Then I talked with an older seaman who'd just come back from across the ocean where they were torpedoing many ships out of every convoy. They were desperate for people and I thought it would be the ultimate high to go overseas. Your Coast Guard book was your seaman's identification and once you had it, age wasn't a factor; you could turn your Coast Guard book in for Merchant Marine papers. And I got in legally at the age of sixteen and I've never met another person who got in at sixteen and didn't lie about his age.

My first trip was down to Cuba and all sorts of things happened. The captain and all of the crew got drunk and ran the ship aground. The Coast Guard had to come down with a ocean-going tug to get the ship free. Here I was in high adventure. When I got up to New York they were making up a new convoy heading for Southhampton, England and I went. From then on I travelled constantly with the Merchant Marine. My final trip on the Atlantic was the Murmansk run. We had a convoy of one hundred and eight ships. Twelve got back.

It was a bad trip and we had a six-month rest leave after that. Then I was ready to go out to sea again. I got on the train and went out to San Francisco and signed on board a Victory ship. It was a long haul and instead of being in convoy we were all alone. When the war ended, I was in the harbor at Manila.

Donald K. Schirmer
100

Saudi Arabia
Collection of Don Schirmer

When you're young, time is so long - it seemed then like I was in the war almost all my life.

I went back to Detroit and that's where I started flying. I love to fly - I'm a commercial pilot with multi-engine land and sea rating, and instrument rating. I went to work in Detroit in the dingy old Hudson Motor Company. The only bright side was that I got to drive past the airport everyday. I would stop in and look at the planes and listen to people talk and daydream. I finally got up my nerve and did a test flight and that started it. I could only afford to fly about one hour or so every couple of weeks.

But that's where my life changed again. I ran into a friend who suggested I join the Army. He said there was a new outfit so secret nobody knew about it called the Army Security Agency. They wanted people who had world experience. So I went down to the recruiting office in Detroit, told them all about where I'd been and what I'd done, and now, some forty years later, I'm still thankful to my friend for putting me on to that because I really received some excellent training. It was tough, basic training in intelligence, then communications and two years of Russian and advanced electronics. From there I went to my first assignment which was Fairbanks, Alaska.

In the meantime I got my pilot's license and bought an airplane, a little Taylorcraft. When I got out of the military, Pacific Northern Airlines had a job waiting for me in radio maintenance. I really enjoyed my work but I was a typical

Donald K. Schirmer

Harriet and Don Schirmer's wedding reception in the Moravian Church, Bethel - 1961
Collection of Schirmer family

single young man, always broke, always in debt. One day I saw an ad in the paper. It said, "Wanted: pilots, mechanics, maintenance personnel, Saudi Arabian Airlines, $700 a month tax-free and all living expenses paid." This was in 1953 and I filled out an application and was accepted.

Next thing you know, I was enroute to Jedda, Saudi Arabia. I checked out on their old DC-3s first and then flew a Bristol 170 which hauls thirty-six passengers.

Once we went up to Jedda to retrieve an airplane that had a bad engine. We were ready to take off when all of a sudden they kicked everybody off because the prince had just arrived and wanted the airplane so he could go see his father. When I found out that the prince was a little eleven-year-old boy, that tickled me so much. So then we flew him on to Riyadh. To me kids are the most important people in the entire world. I hurt when I see them hurting and have a great deal of joy when I see a young person who really has it made.

But Saudi Arabia's pretty tough living. There's a lot of things you can and can't do and after two and one-half years it was just about all I could handle. When somebody asked if I'd like to go to work for Lebanese International Airlines, I gave Saudi Arabian Airlines notice and went to Beirut for a year and a half. Beirut was a beautiful city and I really enjoyed it. During the time I was there, I found a little guy about eleven years old out on the streets - all these little kids slept on the sidewalks at night. Kids suffer so much. I'd learned to speak Italian fairly well and I'd learned to speak some Arabic in Saudi Arabia, so I asked this kid, Elie, if he'd like to go to school, and he was excited.

Donald K. Schirmer

I put him in the Salesian school for boys, an Italian boarding school, and he did very well. One of the side benefits was I worked with him on his English for an hour every night for six months so he'd get up to where the other kids were in English class. We'd speak in Arabic while learning English, and I realized later that I had learned to speak Arabic fluently with a Damascan accent.

Then one day a couple of guys from the State Department came to Beirut looking for somebody to fly two Navion measurement planes I was drooling over. They needed a radio technician, an Arabic interpreter and a pilot for this project, and I could fill all three jobs. I was about twenty-eight or twenty-nine then.

After being in the States for a few months working to get familiar with the electronics procedures for special measuring they were doing, I went back to the Middle East for the State Department. We moved the operation to Baghdad and flew from Karachi to Pakistan, up to Ankara, Turkey.

Almost a year later, I was at the Berlin Hotel in Ankara and the survey was finished. I was thinking I would get to go home, when I got a telegram that said, "Obtain visas for Vietnam, Thailand and Cambodia." That was an exciting trip, the longest trip I ever took in my life - from Ankara clear around across the Persian Gulf, across India, clear over to Bangkok. When I took off from Ankara, the weather was kind of raunchy, so we climbed to sixteen thousand feet with no oxygen on board. Near central Turkey there's a big lake called Lake Van. I knew there was an airfield there with a radio homing beacon so I made a descent homing in on that beacon.

From there we went on to Tehran and then to India. For the entire country of India the only map I had was a *National Geographic* map and a couple of radio facilities charts. We had a twelve hour fuel range, and after we'd been flying for about nine hours I'd tune in to a broadcast station on the ADF [automatic direction finder] and the needle would point to wherever it was and we'd just home in, knowing that we were on the right magnetic course. We arrived in Calcutta about 10:30 one night with smog so dense it was a total instrument approach with no instrument approach facilities. From there we took off over Rangoon into Bangkok. Then to Saigon.

Here we had another one of those close shaves that told me God has a plan for my life. We were supposed to stop in Phnom Pehn, Cambodia. We were probably thirty miles out or so and I'd started my descent when I got a call on my radio giving an urgent message from the U.S. Embassy in Thailand that we weren't to land in Phnom Pehn and were to return to Bangkok. So I

Donald K. Schirmer

turned back to Bangkok and found out that the Cambodians had just machine-gunned an American DC-3 on the ground, killing everyone. This was in 1959 and I had been about to land at that sucker.

From there we took our operation to Saigon. I was there for about thirty days flying demonstration flights for the Vietnamese government and that ended my tour overseas. I had been six years overseas and I was tired of it.

A few weeks later I quit when they wanted to send me back to Bangkok, and the same day I saw an ad for the White Alice System in Alaska. They needed an electronics technician and I ended up in various places like supervisor at Tin City on the Bering Sea where you can look over and see the mountains of Russia. During that time I broke my toes which led to my meeting Harriet.

While I was in Nome getting my broken toes set, they told me that I was being transferred to Bethel. I was excited. Bethel was town, with churches, with people. And that's where I met my wife. She was a doctor and I needed a follow-up x-ray for my foot. So we were happily married and a sparkling little son came along about a year and two months later.

There were a lot of wonderful people in Bethel. Let's face it, Bethel is not really a tropical paradise, but we enjoyed it very much. I was commander of the Civil Air Patrol out there and flew a lot of missions and had a lot of adventures searching for people.

Harriet and their son Jack in their Temco Twin Navion D-16,
Bethel, Alaska 1963
Collection of Schirmer family

We used to fly out to New York every year in our little plane. We left Bethel in 1965 and bought a farm in western New York so we could be close to Harriet's mother. I was known as "Green Acres." I'd come home from work in a business suit and tie and have maybe forty-five minutes to plow before dinner. I had a nice big new tractor so I'd hop on in my suit and start plowing. One day a guy stopped and was standing outside his pickup with a big grin on his face. I stopped and asked if I could help him. "No," he said, "I just had to stop and look. I've always heard of gentlemen farmers but this is the first time I ever saw one." I'd come in to the feed store and they'd say "Here's old Green Acres."

Harriet loves medicine and loves helping people. Consequently she was working sixteen and eighteen hours a day every day. I saw no relief in sight and knew if she kept this up it would kill her. So I decided we'd come back to Alaska.

We looked all around and decided we wanted to be on the water. We heard they needed a doctor in Wrangell and when we came down to look, we discovered we had friends here and decided to stay. That was in 1970, so we've been here twenty-one years now.

We retired a couple of years ago. We wanted to retire while we were young enough to go out and do things. We volunteered last year on the Navaho Indian Nation at Genado, Arizona for a month. Harriet worked in the hospital and I played the organ at the Genado Presbyterian Church and we thoroughly enjoyed it.

We were looking forward to teaching at the English Language Institute of China when Mongolia opened up for the very first time and that seemed about the most far-out place in the world. They asked us if we'd consider going there instead, and Harriet and I looked at each other and almost unanimously said, "Yeah, why not?" We're leaving this year. We'll be teaching English as a Second Language at the agricultural college in Ulaan Baator, Mongolia. And after Mongolia, I would like to go somewhere right in our own country where people need you. I have a gift of music and I'm meant to share it.

I've had a lot of experiences in my life and my greatest pleasures have been helping someone out when I felt that there wasn't anyone else to help them. I've got a lot of young people started off in the aviation business by teaching them flying. And one of the nice things is later on in life when you get a call from one of these young people and they say, "You were the one that got me started."

I love helping young people. I would like to be remembered as a good man, as somebody that loved people and helped them. Most of all, I'd like to be remembered as somebody that loved God.

Donald K. Schirmer

Eva Merrifield

Barrow - The bright March sunlight deceives me and I bundle up for a walk, only to go a short distance and return. My face is numb from the wind off the Arctic Ocean. Eva speaks quietly, in a gentle voice.

I was born in Nome, but moved away when I was four or five. There was Mom and Dad, two grandmas, myself, my brother who was thirteen months younger and my baby sister.

Nome was a segregated community and Dad didn't want us growing up in a segregated community with a school for whites and a school for Natives. So he built a log cabin out in the wilderness along a river, near Moses Point. The two grandmas had their own little log house and we had ours. We lived subsistence. In the springtime, Dad would take us out egg hunting and we'd go Shaktooluk way, to Cape Denby and Cape Darby. The whole family would go and it was wonderful to have fresh eggs. Then in the fall we'd have geese and ducks.

We must have lived there two years and then when Mom was expecting another baby, we moved down to Unalakleet which was her village and where both grandmas came from. I would have been seven at that time. It was very good to have two grandmas. They were wonderful teachers.

At that time in Unalakleet, the population was about four hundred people. Unalakleet means "the windy or stormy place" because the wind blows constantly. It could be gentle breezes or powerful winds.

The church there was a Covenant church with a minister from Sweden. He was wonderful. He didn't just preach on Sunday. He taught gardening and that cleanliness was next to godliness and that we had to have clean houses and clean yards. I thought other places were like our village which was so clean and where we were able to grow our two tons of potatoes. By the time I became a teen, there were two brothers and three sisters, so there were six of us in the family along with the two grandmothers and Mom and Dad. There were some families that were larger, but we were a good-sized family.

The grandmothers were really important. Elders were really important. We got to go camp with them and learn from them. They had a lot of wisdom and

106

they would talk to us. We would pick berries and then have a break and look at the clouds and they'd teach us how to read the clouds so we'd be able to predict the weather. So when I got to Sheldon Jackson and took general science, it was easy because the grandmothers had already taught us a lot. They would tell us stories that had a moral tone. If they wanted to talk about honesty, there was a story that they told. They were much like AEsop's fables. So we were being taught things unawares. At the time, we thought it was just a good story. In the story times, they were teaching about integrity and honesty and saying that we were a culture that had been around for centuries.

Grandmother* spoke archaic Eskimo that was about twenty-five thousand years old. And that was to make sure that when they passed on the oral tradition, it was correct, because the current language was changing. I treasured the camp outs and the egg hunting. They were always talking and giving us tools for adulthood and stressing that I must learn as much as I can to help our people move from the old culture to a culture in transition.

Dad's name was Frank A. Degnan. He was mayor in Unalakleet for about thirty years and he studied the congressional laws and used those laws so we could have better schools, water and sewer. He made many trips to Juneau. He utilized American Indian laws that hadn't been used in Alaska. And he'd talk about this with us and made us listen.

Later on, we had a radio and Dad always made sure we listened to the news. I remember Grandma* would talk to us before the news came on and say something was going to happen. Then we'd listen to the news and she'd be right. She would tell about what was happening in Iwo Jima and other parts of the world. We just thought it was what grandmothers did. And then she'd tell us about things that were going to come about, like man landing on the moon, and that the Eskimos had already been out in the universe to learn more things and that they had sent their people out to observe other countries. And so when I took history in high school, again different areas were familiar and I thought, "How did my grandmother* know these things?" She didn't read, she didn't speak English.

Grandmother* was an only child and came from a line of chieftains, so she had to learn the male role and the female role. She had to be the best hunter, and know her astronomy so she could travel by the stars. She had to know her different kinds of snow. She herself has taken dog sled trips to other villages. She knew about Sitka - her father and grandfather had traded with the Tlingits.

Her husband came up with the Gold Rush in '98. She told us the Eskimos had known about the minerals and the value of them and left them in the

Eva Merrifield's mother, Ada Degnan
Collection of the Merrifield family

ground because they knew if they used them, the life style would change and there would be greed. When we'd go berry picking, she would lift a tussock and soak a cloth in oil seepage to get a fire started. And then she'd tell us not to tell anyone that this is how we light our fires or they would come and ruin the land. She said we needed to keep our environment intact because if one part was messed up, it affected the whole chain of life, whether it was the birds, the plants, or human beings.

But she said change was going to come and then she would weep. She said we would be children of transition and that the Eskimo culture as she knew it would disappear. She would then say, along with my mom and dad, that I would have to go away to school so that I could handle the transition and work with the Native people during the transition from the traditional culture to a changing culture. They were telling me this when I was five or six and it seemed like before I knew it, the time had come to go away to school. I had turned fourteen.

There were three Eskimos attending the Sheldon Jackson Presbyterian boarding school in Sitka and the rest were Tlingit, Haida and Tsimshian. They would tease us but grandma had warned us that this would happen, and that once they got to know us it would be OK. It's not the people that are the enemy, it's just ignorance. And once people learn, problems are resolved.

In Sitka, school was very intense. Academics were half day and then you worked half day. They didn't have a large staff so the students did a lot of the work. It was very good training. We did cleaning, we worked in the library and in the laundromat and we learned industrial cooking. So it was vocational as well as academic.

Eva Merrifield

I got out of school in 1950 and went to work in a hospital. I had scholarships to a school in Washington and Missoula, Montana, but I thought I wanted to be a nurse. I found out later that it wasn't so glamorous and I didn't have the stomach for it. And then I fell in love and figured I could go to college later.

I seems like time went by really fast. I became the mother of five children. We had some good times and we had some sad times and when alcohol entered our lives, it was downhill. Alcohol is very destructive and it's glamorized. People who are not addicted have no idea how destructive it is.

We were taught by our parents and grandparents not to divorce, to do everything you could to make your marriage work. But it doesn't work if it's only one side getting the help, so eventually my husband and I split up. I was still in Sitka. The only place I felt that I could work was at the Mount Edgecumbe School because I wanted my home to be a home for the boarding students who didn't have relatives. It took about six weeks for me to get work and that meant applying for welfare. My parents and grandparents had said, "Find work. Don't get on the system where you get something for nothing." But I finally applied. You do things for your children. You have to put away your pride. And it was just something to bridge the gap.

I worked in Sitka until '64 and then I fell in love again. There were six of us and we came as a package deal. I resigned from my job at the dormitory because he was a fisherman and we were going to Pelican. We got there and I didn't realize the place was so small. We were in Pelican for two-and-one-half years, and I had another child from that marriage. There was no middle of the road there. You could either be a drunk or go to church. Sometimes the winters got very long.

Then the kids and I left and went back to Sitka and I went back to work at Mount Edgecumbe. Then I got married again and in 1968 the kids and I moved to Kenai. What a shock for my children. It was so cold, and only little trees. It was an oil boom town and very wild, so later, when there was a chance to buy property in Seward, we moved over there.

I'd always wanted to work in a cannery. When I was going to Sheldon Jackson, students there were so wealthy. Their parents fished and then the kids worked in the cannery and made good money. And they'd talk about how much fun it was to work in a cannery and it sounded so glamorous and wonderful. So in Seward I went to work in a cannery and it was the hardest work of my life. It was such repetitious work. People were underpaid and would get sick because you're working with cold water. It was mostly women, so we talked and found out that the plant was giving low pay. We asked them for a raise but they

Eva Merrifield
110

Unalakleet
The Ethel Oliver Ross
Collection, University of
Alaska Fairbanks Archives

thought that was audacious of us. The only union that would look at us was
Seafarer's, the others thought we were just small stuff. We finally got union-
ized, but it divided the workers and there were threats to my children. Later,
the union took hold and now they have Teamsters and it's much more fair.

In the 70s we moved up to Anchorage. I wanted the children to be in a
less prejudiced environment. In Seward, the only drunks that got jailed were
the Natives, even though the non-natives were just as drunk. When I got the
children settled in school, I had all this time and I could go to college. It was so
exciting. I went for three years and then the kids and I were on our own again
and I had to leave college.

My daughter was called a "salmon cruncher" on the school bus. Then it
was O.K. to do this to the Natives. That was when I joined PTA and other task
forces. Growing up, we were told that we were not to complain or tear down
leadership, but get in there, find a group and help make the changes. Don't
just condemn, offer your services.

My dad was very active in the land claims movement, going back and
forth to Congress, so in between college in Anchorage, I wanted to help. I got to
meet a lot of wonderful people by just transporting them here and there when
they came in from the bush. I was a quiet person, not at all like my dad who
could speak before thousands of people and go to battle. I got to work for the
Cook Inlet Native Association and that was a very good place because their
target group was the Native population. I became a counselor and when the
Johnson O'Malley program came they wrote it up so that the counselors and
tutors were placed in the actual school sites. I got to make home visits with
Native families and work with the Native kids and try to prevent them from
dropping out.

The process was very slow because I followed the teachings of my grand-

Eva Merrifield

parents and parents. They had said, "Don't forget the circle - the spiritual, mental, emotional, and physical. If one gets out of whack, it throws all the others out, so you have to work in all four areas." It was a really exciting adventure. You got to go to work with the families and find out their needs. Teachers, psychologists, parents - we all became a team working to keep a kid in school.

The Cook Inlet Native Association provided services to the largest Native community in the state, the ten thousand Natives in Anchorage. We had the highest drop-out rate, the most rape victims, the highest unemployment. One year eight Native women were murdered. We wondered why one Native group was so victimized, why was it happening? It seemed really important to me to get on different task forces, boards and commissions to talk about these problems and maybe come to some resolutions. It was a good tool to use instead of sitting back and condemning the system without taking any action. We've got to find our niche and get in there and be part of the solution and not part of the problem. There were a lot of good people willing to work.

Things are going to be better for my children. I think the hardest job of my life was job hunting in Anchorage because it was eight hours a day, five days a week and I would be up in the top three applicants and never get hired. Then my son would wonder if maybe I wasn't any good because I wasn't working. I finally got a job at McLaughlin Youth Center and the runaway shelter. Meanwhile, I kept looking because they don't pay very well in those jobs. Kids are not a real high priority in our system. They don't have the economic base that the oil companies have, so they're last thought of and first defended. And yet they are our most precious resource - if we don't take care of them we won't have a future. At the runaway shelter there were all races of children, and all so needy. And a lot of them were "throwaways" because their parents didn't want them anymore.

And I'd keep looking for another job, keep interviewing. It was a learning experience but it was one of the hardest times of my life. So demoralizing and degrading.

When my little girl, who was five years old, was sexually abused by my husband, the child psychologist said he would be a witness. On the way to court he said, "Are you married to a White or a Native?" I said, "That's a really strange question." He said it was really important to him to know. When I said I was married to a White, he said, "I'm not touching this with a ten-foot pole. All you Natives do incest anyway." And there was my little girl with us and the two of us thought the world had just caved in on us.

Later my fifteen-year-old daughter was raped. The men had covered her with dirt thinking she was dead, and left her. So I got on the Standing Together Against Rape board in Anchorage because they were really trying to do something worthwhile. Thank God for organizations and people working together.

We're still a culture in transition and there's lots of things we need to learn, and we need the help of loving and caring people. When I say that, I mean that when Native people have credentials to teach, hire them. Don't keep them unemployed. There are wonderful talents that are under utilized. Change is too slow, mainly because there is a breakdown in education. Compare the educational system in Greenland and Canada, where they've taught the Natives trilingually. They've had education for over one hundred and fifty years and they've had Native lawyers and civil engineers and other professions for a long time. In Alaska, you can count maybe twelve lawyers? Quite a few teachers, but not too many Natives with a Ph.D.

There is no such thing as retirement in the Eskimo culture. We're supposed to just keep working and doing our thing. I feel it's a privilege to be working as a social worker in Barrow, in a rural population. I hope society utilizes Native elders and doesn't say you can't be hired because you're seventy-five. I think elders have a lot to contribute, they're very stable and they have vast knowledge. Somehow we should be able to teach the younger generation, be mentors and have internships, just like they did in ancient times.

I think people are afraid to learn new things. They think they know it all and don't need to learn anything else. With our family, learning was ongoing and exciting and they made us participants from the smallest to the eldest. Each of us had an important slot. You were put on this earth to do something.

How can the Native people go forward? Get the elders involved with the people. Teach values. We don't live in isolation, we are all members of the human race and we should be able to give dignity and fair chances to one another. I know we need to take care of our problems, but we need help. We need to start with family members and community. But once we work through that process we should have equal opportunities. Native kids still suffer from prejudice in the Anchorage schools. There are some changes being made, but it's so slow. There's a shortage of role models. It's so frightening to have such a high suicide rate among young Native men and to have the high Native incarceration with only fifteen percent of the population. I think there's hope if we all work together to find solutions through the schools, the university, the business community. We can change things.

* Eva's father's mother

Eva Merrifield

Joseph E. Usibelli

For the interview we sit in his office at his hangar in Fairbanks. He's transferring old flight logs to his computer. Mining, airplanes, boats, computers, paintings and science fiction - we talk of many things - his imagination stretching with depth and humor.

The nice thing about being an individual is that there is nobody else anywhere in the universe exactly like you. I think that who you are is partially shaped by the fact that you're short or tall or fat or skinny. It influences you because it influences the people around you. Your personality affects other people and then the way they react to you reflects your personality. The time and the place you live also help to shape you; the people around you certainly do. I know in my own life there have been maybe a dozen people that were very, very important in the way I have developed into a human being.

My father certainly is the first one that comes to mind. He was a very strong person and I loved him dearly. I admired him because he did an awful lot in his life, mostly on sheer guts. He was born in Italy before the turn of the century and came to this country when he was fourteen. The whole family was extremely poor. They came to an environment that had a lot more opportunity, but really wasn't much better as far as living conditions. When he left Italy he'd only had three years of schooling, the only formal education he ever had. He was a self-educated person and had an extremely good memory so anything that he saw he learned from. He was more knowledgeable than most of the highly educated people that I've met.

I could go on about my father a long time. He's the one that really started it all and he did it from absolutely nothing but a lot of hard work and a belief that he could do it. That's the biggest thing if you want to succeed: thinking you can succeed. If you really believe you can do something, you can do something. And if you do not think you can do it, you won't be able to do it. It's all from within. And I'm not talking just about business, I'm talking about everything, absolutely everything. A lot of people blame outside influences, and there are outside influences, but in the long run, if you think you can do something, you can do it.

My father and mother came up in '35 before I was born. They came up to

Joe Usibelli with his parents and younger sister, Rosalie 1945.
Collection of the Usabelli family

work in the mine down at Matanuska. They stayed there about a year and then they worked for Cap Lathrop at the Healy River coal mine. My father worked there until sometime in '37 just before I was born. Then he broke his back in an underground mining accident. The standard for companies at that time was that if someone was injured on the job, as soon as they healed up enough to work, they worked them long enough to prove that they were able to work and then they fired them to alleviate the ongoing liability. But my father was such a hard worker that while this was their policy, they also really didn't want to lose his talents, so they gave him a contract to cut timber for the mine and he became a logger in that area. Then in '43, after the war had broken out, the military bases were growing rapidly and there was a need for coal. He was able to get the lease on some federal property adjacent to the Healy River property and started his own mining operation. And it just kind of grew from there.

There were years when there were no contracts and things were very tight. And I guess we were very, very poor. I didn't know it at the time. I don't remember being deprived of anything that was important. In those days, there was no television so nobody was high pressuring you. It was a wonderful place to grow up. It was a very, very small community but there were a lot of other kids and we were right there in the woods. I don't think there was a finer place to grow up in the world than in Alaska at that time. I guess a lot of that is ignorance. You don't know what things are like anywhere else so you don't have anything to compare them too.

My father was a very dynamic person and worked very hard all his life and enjoyed everything he did. He had a fantastic sense of humor, and a good sense of the ridiculous. There are so many ridiculous things in this world that you just have to be amused by and I think that's the thing a lot of people miss. You really can't take yourself too seriously, you know. If you can't laugh at yourself, you're missing one of the greatest sources of humor you're ever going to find. Half the humor in my life is just stupid things that I've done. We all do a lot of ridiculous things, the world does, the politicians; you look at it and you better be able to laugh or it's going to kill you.

My father was like me in that I don't really set a lot of very specific goals. You just kind of go with the flow and take advantage of whatever the situation is. You go the direction that becomes apparent at the time.

I think that people take themselves and humanity too seriously. They don't look at the big, broad picture. We're just a little blip here on this world. They say

Early Usibelli coal mine truck
Collection of Usibelli Coal Mine, Inc.

Joe Usibelli, three years old.
Collection of the Usibelli family

Joseph E. Usibelli

the earth is about a billion and a half years old, and civilized mankind has only been on it about the last five thousand years. That's nothing, absolutely nothing. It's one of the problems we have now with the excessive government controls and the environmental movement. You've really got to look at it from a long perspective. People get excited and tear their hair and run around in circles and say, "The sky is falling, the sky is falling," but we don't know that. And we won't know that for the next hundred thousand years. So a person's lifetime is minuscule and probably fairly meaningless.

Obviously, to me mankind is extremely important. But in the overall scheme of things it's not. And that bothers some people. It doesn't bother me. So what? So I'm not important to the cosmos, I'm important to me. I'm important to my family. I'm important to a lot of people. And that's all that's really necessary.

I was very fortunate. I had parents who were excellent people, both very bright, very caring, thinking people. A lot of youth today suffer from not having support from their parents and that's too bad. Raising kids is a very important thing and unfortunately we all do it as amateurs. I suppose what really should surprise us is that so many people turn out very well, rather than very badly. Certainly my immediate family has been a big influence on my life. And in the process of teaching children you probably learn more than you teach.

And there have been a few people that I've been associated with in business and my career that I've learned a lot from. Most of those were employees. The most successful people that I've seen in business, people able to go the direction they want to go, get along well with their people and recognize that people are people. Whether it's the guy sweeping the floor or the most important job in the company, they're still just people. And you can get the most production from them if you understand them. You've got to use people for what they are best suited. And that philosophy has worked for us very well. It attracts good people and keeps them. We have some of the best people in the world. And they're the most productive people.

I grew up in Healy until 1950 and then one of the events that shapes your life occurred. My folks got divorced and my mother and sister and I moved into Fairbanks. I was eleven years old and just getting ready to start eighth grade and the school in Healy did not include a high school. So it was a good time for me to get out of a one-room school situation and into the "big city" of Fairbanks.

Then I went to the University of Alaska and graduated in '59. Like any kid, I was going to be five hundred different things before I grew up but I just kind of gravitated back to the mine. I graduated from college as a civil engineer and then went to Stanford for a couple of quarters in '63 and '64 for mechanical

Joseph E. Usibelli
118

Joe Usibelli views the Suntranna Tipple site where coal trains were loaded between 1922 and early 1980's
Collection of the Usibelli Coal Mine, Inc.

engineering, but I think probably the ultimate degree is one that very few universities offer and that's a basic engineer. The engineer's basic function is to simplify: to create order out of chaos. And that puts you in pretty good shape for business because it's the same kind of thinking. You have to take all the many variables and get them assembled in some kind of order that makes sense. And I think that's basically what I've always tried to do - make simplicity out of complication.

I've always found mining fascinating because it's complex. Of course, everything is more complex than it appears. But mining is extremely complex because you get to work in so many different areas. It never gets boring. There are never any two days the same. And the real fun is when things aren't going right: when they're chaotic and they're a lot of hard work. But you look back on them and say, "Boy, I really enjoyed that." Particularly if you can come to a successful conclusion - chaos is very exciting.

When things get into a routine I go nuts. I'm basically a builder. I like to create new things. To start off with something and just run it doesn't do much for me. But to take something and improve it and expand it and make it larger, or better, or more efficient - that's what it's really all about. Creative business you don't do with rules. You do it by taking chances, by doing things people tell you can't be done, or shouldn't be done, or aren't needed and proving them wrong.

A lot of people try to run their businesses by the book. Advances are always made by the person who is told, "You can't do that," and who goes ahead and does it. I call it the bumblebee theory. Theoretically you ask an aeronautical engineer, "Can a bumblebee fly?" and the answer is "No, he can't. His body mass is too large for his wing area." But nobody told the bumblebee,

Joseph E. Usibelli
119

so he goes ahead and flies anyhow. And that's kind of the way it has to be. Every accomplishment, every step that has been a major step forward has always had somebody there saying, "No, no, no. You can't do that. It's too dangerous. It's too risky. It can't be done. You shouldn't do that." And I've generally chosen to ignore that. Some steps were steps backwards. But then you learn from that and go some other way and ultimately you will succeed.

You always have your doubts and you're never sure if you're going to be there next year. There were many times when things were awfully tight and we didn't know if we would continue to exist. Even now, if people came up with cold fusion and they didn't need coal anymore, we wouldn't have a job. You're never sure what's going to happen tomorrow. That's the one thing you want to keep in your mind in absolutely anything. People who strive for total security are never going to get it. And, I can't really imagine why they would want it. I don't want to know what's going to happen tomorrow. It's too exciting finding it out as it comes along.

I'm very fortunate that my sons, and my whole family really, have taken an interest in the mine, are working in it and are very successful at it. I could feel it at the time, but I've read since, that a person in the chief executive spot should not be there more than twenty years because after that time you've kind of run out of ideas. It's time for some new blood to come in. And it has proved to be true. It's been almost five years now since my son took over and things are better now than they ever were. I think they feel at times that I don't care because I'm not there as much. But I'm not there because I do care. Because you really can't have two bosses. There comes a point where you've just got to let go and say, "O.K. kid, it's yours."

People say, "Are you middle aged?" Well, I'm certainly middle aged. How many people do you know live to be a hundred? I'm well into middle age. And that's fine. There are some real advantages. You can start really speaking your mind and get away with it. Things that if you said them as a kid, you'd be rude, but you get a few gray hairs and they think, "Oh, those are words of wisdom." But they're the same words. Kids have a lot of insight. You really need to pay attention to what they say.

The greatest thing that ever happened to me were my kids. I think of all the things that I've accomplished, and I can give you a list of supposed accomplishments, the only ones that were really important were the kids. Because I guess that's your immortality. Also, probably the toughest job you'll ever have is raising children well. And just looking at the results I can say, "Yeah, we've done a good job." I certainly can't take a whole lot of the credit. I have to give most of

Joseph E. Usibelli

120

that to my wife. My wife was a very big influence on me. A very positive one. We've been together a long time and we've grown together, learning from each other and learning from the situation. But it's the most satisfaction to watch those kids grow up and turn into real, honest-to-god, responsible adults. The most important thing that anybody can do in life is to leave the world a little bit better than it was when you came into it. And there are a lot of ways of doing that and I think that I've done that in a few ways, but the kids that you leave behind are probably the most lasting.

There's an awful lot of opportunity here. I think that somebody wanting to make a difference probably has a better opportunity to do it in Alaska than any other place because there's going to continue to be rapid growth in Alaska. You're in an area where things are changing very rapidly and everybody is significant. We've been going through some economic hard times lately and the biggest reason is we have become way too dependent on one single industry. The

A backhoe sitting on top of a 25 foot coal seam
loads one of the mine's haul trucks.
Collection of the Usibelli Coal Mine, Inc.

other problem is that we still do not have control of our destiny, politically. Probably the biggest mistake that we made is in becoming a state instead of becoming a country.

You'll find that the average miner knows about the environment. He goes out there and lives in it every day. Our industry, because of media coverage or media bias has a bad reputation which is not deserved. And there have been bad areas of the country, but on the whole you'll find that most miners care a lot. We have to live here too. In the past there've been a lot of things that went wrong out of ignorance. It's a matter of perspective. We are learning things. We are more able to do the right thing now because we've got the tools to do it, which we didn't have before. I can take you to areas that we mined thirty years ago and you can't tell that we've been there. Not because we did anything to it, but because it heals itself up. Nature heals pretty well.

And you're really better off focusing on your immediate environment. Because there you can have some effect and I really doubt that anybody, right up to the president or anyone else, can have as big an effect as he thinks he has on the overall scope of things. Things will happen more in spite of us than because of us. If we could all kind of worry about our own little backyard and take care of that, I think we'd all be much better off.

One of the things that brings people to Alaska is the beauty of the place. Everybody needs a little beauty in their lives. With music, art and many other aesthetics, people just need the time and background to appreciate them. My mother is an artist and did a lot of painting, so I got an early introduction. And looking at some of the graffiti in the inner cities you can see this innate need for people to express themselves. It's just part of the human soul.

It has been my observation that everyone makes their decisions based on emotions rather than thought. And I think that's the right thing to do. Particularly in a business situation or industrial situation, you never have enough data to make a decision. And there are some people who can't make a decision without all the data so they keep putting off the decision and they continue to gather more and more data and by the time they get all their data, there's no decision left to make. On the other hand, if you take an intuitive approach, and say O.K., based on the information I have, my hunch is that this is the way to go, the average person is going to be right ninety percent of the time. People are afraid they're going to make mistakes so they don't do things. My feeling is that O.K., so I make a mistake, it's no big deal. So I might as well go ahead and try.

I just kind of live from day to day. I really do. I don't know what tomorrow's going to bring. I'm not a great one for making plans, I'm very much more a spur-

Joseph E. Usibelli
122

of-the-moment person. That doesn't always work. I can't say that I really recommend that to anybody because it does make life somewhat chaotic and there are some things well beyond your control that you really just have to plan around. But it's the attitude that tomorrow is tomorrow and what it brings, I'll enjoy that too, or not, as the case may be. And if not tomorrow, then there's the day after that, too. Because I'm pretty sure I'm immortal. People say, "Well, you're not immortal and you should plan for that." I don't think so. Obviously, we are all of us mortal, but you ought to live as if you were immortal. It makes life a lot more enjoyable.

Joe Usibelli stands in front of the mine's 2,000 ton drag line which is used to uncover coal seams.
Collection of the Usibelli Coal Mine, Inc.

Edith Bullock

Anchorage - "She always looked like she just stepped out of Vogue," is the first thing I heard about Edith and her days in Kotzebue. When I met her in her Anchorage condo, she was a tiny woman, still elegantly dressed.

It's pretty hard to capsulize fifty years of living in Alaska in a few words. I was born in 1903. I kept that a secret for a number of years, but now that I have become the age that I am, I've begun to brag about it. I was thirty-three when I came to Nome in 1939 on the Alaska steamship *Denali*. Most of the passengers on this ship were Filipinos, who disembarked at Dutch Harbor, to be flown out to work in the different canneries. It was not until I was in the legislature many years later that I understood that the Alaskan fishing industry was dominated by financial interests in Seattle. These outside interests came up here - putting in their own canneries and importing their own people - with all of the profits and products, including the payroll, going back outside.

When we got into Nome, the ship anchored about a mile off shore as the water was too shallow for it to dock. Everything had to be off-loaded from the ship to the lighter, that's a scow, which was then towed ashore by a small tug. They put the steps down the side of the ship and we went down to this lighter and all huddled in the middle of it. There wasn't really a dock; you just stepped off where they handled the freight. I was so excited as I thought of Nome's history as an old gold rush town. I walked down those old, dirty streets on the board sidewalks and thought I'd come home. I just loved it. I never lost that feeling.

I had been living in Seattle, recently divorced, and I was eager to change my way of living. I thought how great it would be to come to Alaska. But in the 1930s there really wasn't much work up here, and you were advised not to come unless you had enough money to get back to Seattle if you couldn't find a job. Incidentally, in those days there was what they called a "blue ticket" that they gave to people that were undesirables, who they wanted to get rid of. They would give them this "blue ticket" and send them back Outside.

I had an aunt and uncle in Nome, and I wrote them of my desire to come

up. They wrote back that there was a position as a bookkeeper for a mining company about forty miles out of Nome. The Lee Brothers Dredging Company operated a couple of dredges on the Solomon River and I spent the summer down there, coming into town for the winter on Thanksgiving day. I can still vividly remember that fall. Hundreds of caribou cut through the camp, crossing the Solomon River on their way to new grazing grounds, and wolves howling at night as they caught the scent of the female dog in the camp.

There were lots of parties in Nome in the winter and we had a wonderful time because a new woman was always interesting to the male population.

My second year there I was married. Jack had been in Nome for quite awhile and was working for the mining company as dredgemaster. Then the second world war came along and Jack was taken into the army and was an Alaskan Scout for three of his four years. When he got out we went into mining for ourselves up at Teller. Then we went trapping over in the Upper Salcha country for the winter. And that was a marvellous experience.

We came back to Teller for the mining season, with Jack and his partner Chuck O'Leary going back and trapping the second winter. While they were gone, Wien [Wien Air Alaska] needed an office manager at Kotzebue and I was sent up to take over. And I found it the most intriguing place. The characters in Kotzebue were just endless and absolutely unique. It was a Native town dominated by white traders and was completely different. I loved it. Jack joined me when he came back from trapping and we decided we'd make Kotzebue our home. That was in 1948.

In the meantime, we had acquired a dredge up in the Kougarok Mountains and we went up the summer 1950 and mined there. The dredge operated around the clock from mid-April until the first of October. I cooked for the crew and I never got so sick of anything in my life. We were really isolated. Supplies were usually dropped from a plane into camp, but if we had something that had to be off-loaded, then we had to take the tractor and "go-devil" (wooden sled) over the tundra to the little airfield, which was about three miles away. Gold mining isn't easy, but there's the greatest satisfaction when you look in your pan, or in your boxes from the dredge, and you see some gold in there. In that part of the country there were not too many nuggets, and not exactly flakes either, but fine gold. Gold comes in all different forms. Mining is exciting and it can really grab you. There's a tremendous feeling of accomplishment.

That was the year the Korean War started and we realized we were going to have difficulty getting parts. We had only marginal ground so we decided we'd have to do something else.

Edith Bullock
126

I went back to Kotzebue and Jack stayed at the camp to get everything put away and tightened up for winter. On his way back he stopped and talked to Grant Jackson, president of the Miner's and Merchant's Bank of Nome, about his idea to start an oil distribution business in Kotzebue. And as a result, in 1951 we got into the tug and barge freighting business in competition with Archie Ferguson.

Archie had a store in Kotzebue. He had the movie house, the restaurant, a flying business - everything, including a tug and barge lightering and fuel business. He was probably the best-known character in the north. He was completely without an ethical approach to anything. It was "buyer beware." There was no meanness in Archie, everything was a game with him. He had a great sense of humor as long as whatever was going on wasn't against him. Archie and the Eskimos, who are top-notch traders themselves, had a great thing between them, with Archie coming out on top most of the time. Archie had used "bingles" (wooden tokens) to pay people off when they worked for him. These, of course, were good only in Archie's establishments. Then when "bingles" were outlawed, anybody who worked for Archie received credit in "the book" and could trade against it. No money ever changed hands - there was no cash in Kotzebue. No one could cash a check, there was not a bank.

The Internal Revenue Service finally got interested in Archie as they were sure he was not paying his proper taxes. But they couldn't prove it, because Archie had no records. He had a flour sack, and he would just stuff in invoices and bills, and every once in awhile he would throw it away. It took six or seven years before they had sufficient evidence to close him down, and Archie lost everything.

In the spring of 1951, we had three steel bulk barges built at Blaine, Washington, and we bought a tug. We had a partner for a short time, a Kotzebue trader, Louis Rotman, and if it hadn't been for his support and help we might not have made it. Louis was well known in the wholesaling area in Seattle and was able to get supplies and all sorts of credit. We knew we had a tough operating period ahead and we didn't know a darn thing about the marine freighting business. It was called the B & R for Bullock and Rotman.

Jack sold Standard Oil of California on the need for bulk tanks in Kotzebue - the first bulk tanks in the Arctic - and they built three tanks, one for motor oil, one for stove oil and one for diesel. We then delivered oil supplies to eleven villages on the different rivers.

All petroleum products and freight had to be lightered about twelve miles because the water is so shallow. There are two great rivers that go past

Edith Bullock

127

Edith outside of her office in
Kotzebue 1966
Collection of Edith Bullock

Loading oil drums to take home -
Kotzebue 1960
Collection of Edith Bullock

Pulling in loaded barge - Kotzebue 1956
Collection of Edith Bullock

Kotzebue, the Kobuk and the Noatak, and the silt fills in. That's one reason there's so much cost to the freighting; you have to have it handled more than once.

We hired all Eskimos in our operation and many of them used the money they made with us to buy stove oil and gasoline. They all wanted an oil stove. Otherwise they had to spend most of the winter scavenging around getting wood. Also the rivers are the highways of rural Alaska, and gasoline is needed for the boats.

From the very beginning of our business, we shipped cash in from Nome and paid our employees off in cash because if we'd given them checks they couldn't have cashed them. We did that until finally we got a bank into Kotzebue in 1960. The natives didn't know anything about handling money because they never had any. It was a barter/subsistence system.

When Louis Rotman wanted out in 1952, I took over his interests and Jack and I became equal partners. I'm very practical and Jack was a visionary. He could see all sorts of possibilities. With the Black Navigation Company he got Yutana Barge Lines servicing the Yukon River, with headquarters in Nenana. He was also responsible for getting the government to open up bidding for the large DEW line supply to private bidders. As a result he was away a good deal while I was there handling the B & R Tug and Barge. It led to an eventual separation and finally a divorce. My part of the settlement was the B & R, which I wanted.

So there I was. It was a tremendously interesting business. Everything was a new experience because it just hadn't been done before. And I was very proud of our operation. Ray Heinrichs was responsible for operations and I handled financing and planning. Our tugboat crews were all Eskimos and it became a matter of pride to work for the B & R. I think part of the success of the company was that we didn't exploit the people. We hired the people of our area, and the money stayed there instead of going out, as usually happened.

The worst, of course, much the worst that ever happened to us, was when we lost a tugboat crew. It was a terrible storm. One of our tugs, towing a barge, was in Nome. Robert Gallahorn, the captain, knew we had a freighter coming in and that we needed them in Kotzebue for lightering. So in spite of storm warnings, he started back north. Apparently the storm worsened, and off Wales, the wind and waves carried the barge up on top of the tug and capsized it. When we were unable to contact the captain by radio, planes were sent out. After three days of searching, the bodies of the three crew members were located on a beach. That was a terrible, terrible thing and it took a long time to get over.

Edith Bullock

When I first went to Kotzebue, the housing conditions were horrible, really horrible. Little huts lined the beach, some of them with sod roofs. Those that were built with plywood and plasterboard were not adequately insulated. It was pretty miserable. The people were getting away from subsistence, but they had little income. There was some help from the government, but it was a very, very, hard life for them.

The non-natives who lived and worked in Kotzebue were conscious that we were in a native village. We didn't want to usurp the rights of the people who lived there. It was a very different experience than in Nome where the discrimination resulted in separation of natives and whites in the movie house, with natives barred from restaurants and many other places. That gradually changed.

I was up there for twenty-one years and most of that time was in building up the B & R. It was all so different then. It was an awful lot of work but I don't think about that so much as I do about the high points and the funny things that happened. And it was a very rewarding experience. I was so deeply involved with everything that it fascinated me. I never made any great plans. I knew in a general way what services were needed and what to expect from customers, and was able to sort of sense what was going to happen and make plans. You have a lot of problems up there. You don't have any infrastructure at all to work with. You just go into a village and you unload freight onto the river bank and if the men aren't there, the women act as longshoremen. We lived and made history.

We were terribly isolated in those days. In Nome we were lucky if we got mail once every three weeks in wintertime. Pan Am flew in with passengers and mail and they were our lifeline to Outside. I've always had a soft spot in my heart for Pan Am because of the kind of service they gave us. It took us two days to get out to Seattle in those days. Everything has changed so completely that it's hard for anyone who didn't live in those days to visualize what it was like. It really was tough. But you didn't think about that. You just had things to do and you did them and I really loved what I did.

As I look back, I realize it took me a great many years to finally reach adulthood, but I learned as I went along and I was just fortunate, very fortunate and I worked awfully hard. I think I used good judgment, generally, and I had a lot of support - my banker, my operations foreman, my friends, and the people themselves, so I couldn't help but make it under the circumstances.

I was in the legislature for six years, including the last three sessions of the territorial legislature. I was tremendously interested in politics. I found it frustrating and completely fascinating and I loved it. When it came to statehood, I

Edith Bullock
130

B & R Tugs pulled out for the winter of 1963-64 Kotzebue
Collection of Edith Bullock

was the only vote against it because my constituents were not in favor of it. I took an awful lot of flak about that. I was wrong because the oil companies came in and made it profitable for us as a state, which they couldn't have done had we remained a territory.

There were times when I wished that I was any place else but the legislature, because you had very difficult issues. Decisions have to be made affecting all the people of Alaska.

I was an extreme conservative when I came to Alaska. The longer I lived in Kotzebue, the more moderate I became. Living with a disadvantaged group of people you see things that can't be understood or accepted. So, you change.

It's just natural for me to be optimistic. And having contacts makes it possible for you to contribute something. I was a director of the Alaska State Chamber for many years, a regent for the University of Alaska for eight years, and served on many other boards. I learned something from everything I got into and I hope that I was contributing something. I think you get out of life what you put into it. Of course I worried about things, but I never let it stop me in any way. I've always been eager to accept anything that might be new and different and try it anyway.

Portions of this biography were taken from oral history tapes in the Archives of the Elmer Rasmuson Library, University of Alaska Fairbanks.

Edith Bullock

131

Helen Rhode

Cooper Landing - The log house is down off the road, sitting right on the water. Inside, looking out the window and across the lake, she points out Cecil Rhode Mountain.

Cecil and I married in Seattle and came up to where he had built a cabin in the 30s. We met in Seattle during the war. Cecil didn't mislead me at all. He wanted me to know what the score was and what kind of life-style we'd have and it was like he had said - pretty simple - wood heat, no electricity, a log cabin, water from the lake. All these things he had explained. Actually, in those days ladies either thoroughly enjoyed it or they didn't like it at all. I thoroughly enjoyed it. I don't know now in my seventies that I would want to go back to it. But in those days, I never gave it a thought. Of course, I was - how old was I when we married? - I was born in 1919, got married in '46, so I wasn't a youngster.

I enjoyed Cooper Landing. It was small. There weren't too many people, so you had friends all the way from their twenties on up. And there were still a lot of the old-timers that had been here since way back at the turn of the century.

While he was working for Boeing Aircraft during the war years, Cecil had shown some of his slides. People enjoyed them and he decided he would like to make a lecture film. So when we returned to Alaska, he spent two or three years making his first wildlife film.

Cecil didn't come back to Alaska just to make a film, he considered Alaska home. He already had a cabin built and was only out during the war years. He'd intended to enlist, but when they learned he had grown up at a watch maker's bench, they said Boeing was in need of instrument men and he worked there until V-J day.

When the film was finished, we took it out on lecture tour until our son was born. As we didn't want to take him on the road, Cecil would drive us from here all the way to Texas and leave us at my mother and dad's. His shows were mostly in the Midwest or the East and then he would come all the way back to Texas to pick us up and drive us home. Most people stayed on the road about six months of the year for the lecture season, but about three months was all

Cec wanted of Chicago, Detroit and those cities. Later, he started doing a little work for Disney. He refused a full-time job, so Disney provided film and Cec shot his own or Disney's and was paid for the footage Disney used. He did work for other television and cinema producers too.

But he never punched a time clock in all the years we were married. He never did anything but photography. When he was out lecturing he made good money, but then we'd have years that we didn't make much. But we lived a simple life-style. It didn't take too much financial support when you could raise a garden, shoot a moose, catch fish, dig clams, pick berries and burn wood. You got your property from the Forest Service, home siting, and you built your own log cabin. We lived in blue jeans and we didn't have a car for three years, so it didn't really take too much.

In the first three years I didn't go out with him on long backpacking trips - only day trips or short overnights. By the time he had his big heavy tripod and movie camera and food and stuff - he would go out for three weeks sometimes - I couldn't keep up with him. I couldn't pack enough. Then we started going on trips in the car to Denali. It was one of the ideal places for photographers - all the animals. At that time you still had to take your car on a flatcar on the train. They unloaded it at the railroad station. I'd get bored just sitting there waiting while he was out working for two or three hours, so he bought me good camera equipment, good lenses. I am still using the same lenses and cameras that he bought me years ago. I enjoyed doing it and enjoyed being with him. In the fall, we'd go up to visit Harry Johnson at his mining claim for moose pictures, and would stay for a month. We would pack in the camera gear. We had a friend who

Helen Rhode
134

had an airplane and he'd fly over and make a drop. Cec had packed everything in five-gallon cans to be tied out on the wings with rope, and our friend would release them. It was up at the high valley above timberline and in those days, the type of things you would take, nothing would break - army surplus food, beans and things like dried fruits. So we didn't have to pack all of that in. Then we would work all the high valleys up there during the fall and the moose rut period.

I still qualify to get my photographer's permit in Denali because I enjoy going back and seeing old friends and meeting photographers. You can go up and work on sheep on the hillside and come back and get in your car, go down the road a mile and there will be caribou, another two miles and there will be moose. So you have a lot of variety there.

The hardest part is marketing, to me. If you write, it helps sell pictures and if you take pictures, it helps your writing, but we almost never did both. Cecil wrote an article for *National Geographic* once on the McNeil River bears, and some articles for the outdoor magazines in the early days. I did one or two, but just to sell some pictures.

For about ten years after Cecil's death, when I would go out to Washington, D.C. to see my mother, I didn't mind the marketing too much, because you could get on the metro and you could get off at *National Wildlife* or *Ranger Rick* or *National Geographic* or the *Smithsonian* or the *National Rifleman*. You could go in and hand the photos to the secretary and say, "Call me when you want me to pick them up." Actually, for the last years, many of the sales were at those places.

I was born in Oklahoma. I moved to Texas about the time I started high school and I went to college in Texas. I actually taught school for a couple of years or so. I liked teaching because I had the summers off. One year I went to the East coast and the other to the West. But during the war years, I went coach on the train and you felt kind of guilty because there were so many soldiers standing up and needing room and trying to get home on furlough. Then I went to work for Braniff Airlines in Wichita Falls as a terminal hostess, not an air hostess. We just had two flights a day. It was war years and the men were in the service so we had to check in the passengers, check in the mail, work the radio and only occasionally had to bring a plane in or push out the ramps. But that was what I was doing when I got married.

Right after the war, in '46, an awful lot of people came to Alaska. You would be surprised how many came here to Cooper Landing. During the war they learned they didn't have to stay around their little home town.

Helen Rhode

It makes a difference when your husband isn't punching a time clock or going to the office. When David was growing up, there would be two or three weeks at a time when he wouldn't see his dad, or if his dad was on a lecture tour for three months at a time. But when his dad was here, they could do anything they wanted to do. They could go fishing, or if Cec was building a cabin, David was trailing right along on his footsteps. They actually had a lot more time together than the average father who comes home at five and the kid goes to bed at eight. They were just inseparable when Cecil was home and in the winter. Most of the winter he didn't do much photography. The animal life was more on the trips in spring, summer and fall. He did hardly any stills - only cinematography. He had the lab out here in which to sit and edit his films and put it together, and then he would get copies, dupes made up, which was quite a job.

We had a lot of time together in the winter. The first years we were married, we were very reluctant to get a snow machine. They were noisy and we thought, "Yuk." But we got one, and actually it opened up a lot of interesting country. In one day's time we could go fifteen, twenty miles back up into high country that we would usually never get into, and then be home. We would go with groups. And we would use snowmachines instead of having to start the car when it was cold and wintery. We'd keep them here on the lake and run down to the post office. We had a lot more ice on the lake in those years. We would go out and cut ice blocks that were three feet thick. We'd help a friend and he would put them in his meat house and cover them with sawdust and they would last almost half the summer. For our water hole we had to cut through two or three feet of ice.

Cecil first came up to float down the Yukon with his brother Leo in 1933. They went steerage to Ketchikan, traded a rifle for a row boat and then came up the Inside Passage. It took them all summer because they had to go with the right weather and tides. He said that every time they came to a fox farm or a lighthouse, people would want them to stay a few days. They made it to Haines. In '34, he floated the Yukon with his cousin Clarence. Cecil came to Kenai Lake in '37 to go hunting and built a log cabin in '38.

When he first came up, it was during the Depression years. He told me the first job he had that first summer was with the CCC [Civilian Conservation Corps]. CCC was a government agency like WPA [Work Projects Administration] - a work corps of some kind. Of course, in those days the interest in Alaska was fishing and if beaver were blocking fish streams the fish couldn't get up to spawn. So their job was to blowup beaver dams. Once, they came into a place south of Juneau. It was too late to work on the beaver dam down the stream, so they made camp. The next morning they went down to their boat and couldn't

Helen Rhode
136

*Cecil Rhode Mountain in
Cooper Landing*
Photo by David Rhode

find one of the oars. It had been worked into the dam overnight.

I didn't worry much about him. He never had close encounters that much. But then, he sort of understood the animals and he never pressed them. He never pushed them. One time he had to shoot a bear. He was out by himself on an open hillside and there was a cluster of trees. As he got close, this bear came out of the brush. She was pretty close to him and there wasn't anything he could do. She turned and went back and she had cubs. In the meantime, he saw a single tree and he climbed it. He did end up having to shoot her, but that was the only time in all those years. But again, he didn't press them, he understood them.

Actually, after we got married he never hunted, except moose. We only ate sheep when friends gave us some. The moose would do us, plus the fish, birds, rabbits, clams and other things. He really didn't like that part of hunting any more. He never trapped or did any of those other things, just photography.

I've never lived anyplace else in Alaska but Cooper Landing. When I came everything was in Seward. That was where you did your shopping. Seward was the hub because there was a road. You couldn't drive to Anchorage or Soldotna, there was no road.

What was fascinating about Cooper Landing when I first came were these old-timers that had been here before the war and way back into the twenties. They came out here before there were any roads and most of them were big game guides. They would have clients from Europe and back East, but in those days they usually went on a month's hunt. Now they come in, hop on an airplane and do it in three or four days. In those days, they all had to come by boat to Seward and then come down the lake and down the river. Most of the guided hunting went on between Skilak and Tustumena and they didn't have powerful enough motors to come back upstream so they would go down to Kasilof to the arm. And a lot of people trapped in those days.

I just want to stay right here in Cooper Landing and continue to do a certain amount of photography and enjoy friends. I wouldn't change anything. I like just the way it's going. I'm happy. I can see where it would be fun to do some traveling, but if I can go to Dawson, I'm happy.

Helen Rhode

137

Ralph Moody

Anchorage - Sitting in his home over tea, one feels far away from courtroom life. But a few minutes of conversation in his slow, mumbling accent and dry humor, and I realize it is still very present with him.

I'll give you my full name. Ralph E Moody. E only. I say "only" because when I was in the service, everytime I put E down, they came back and I fought with them three or four months. I don't have a middle name.

I was born 23 November 1915 in Vance, Alabama. We moved from there when I was six months old and ended up in Georgetown, Alabama, where my dad had decided to farm as a tenant farmer. I started school there. I was born a twin, but my twin brother died when he was five years old. I have just slight recollection of him. I remember the day he got seriously ill and my parents called a doctor and it took about three hours for the doctor to arrive in those days because we were twenty miles from town. But he was obviously seriously ill with convulsions. I recall that my sister and I didn't go to the funeral because it was spinal meningitis and they knew it was catching. So they took me away from the house for a couple of days so they could fumigate it, make sure it was all gone. That's the only memory I have of him.

My sister was ten years older than I. She had just finished high school and they allowed her to teach seven classes in a one-room schoolhouse. And if you don't think you needed discipline there, you don't know kids. You could learn what everybody was learning if you'd listen. I don't recommend it, but I think in those days it was advantageous because we didn't have TV, and telephones and newspapers. If you got in trouble and had to be switched, you had to go out and cut your own switch. If you got it too small, they sent somebody that didn't like you out to get another one. So you were careful not to get in trouble. I never will forget when my sister was told she was going to teach us. Of course, we were very happy because we thought we'd get preference. But our parents told us that if we got into trouble at school, we got in trouble twice at home. We knew they meant it, so she didn't have any trouble with us at all.

I wasn't quite big enough to plow, but I had to help with all the farm duties.

We had pigs and cattle, cows to milk, chickens to feed. My dad finally decided to give up farming after about six or eight years and he started working for a logging company out of a small town about six miles away and we moved down there for about a year. Then he got another job in the turpentine business which he'd been raised up in, back in Vance. He kept that job for many years. But he still had the farm on his mind and he later bought an eighty-acre farm about three miles away from our home. Farming it was quite a chore. In the summertime, I'd go out six days a week, three miles each way, either ride the mule or walk. I did that through high school. It was in the Depression and we had plenty to eat but vegetables and farm products didn't bring too much in those days.

My sister finally bought a home for my mother and dad. They never were able to buy one. She bought it and she moved them there. My dad had bought the eighty-acre farm, but he was living in a rented house.

In my second year in high school, my dad gave me a calf and said "You raise this and you can have it when you get ready to go to college. I probably won't be able to help you otherwise. Maybe you can sell it and get enough to start." This calf became a milk cow, and I rented her out to a neighbor to feed her and get the milk.

With all the money I saved, I went to the University of Alabama, in Tuscaloosa. My brother'd just finished there and he'd worked his way through college. I had some contacts and I got a job as a monitor in the boys' barracks and I got my room for that. I got a job waiting on tables for my meals and working three hours a night in a little cafe for one dollar a night. The second year of doing that, some people in the fraternity house told me that people were selling snacks at night and the guys would tip and I could probably make three or four dollars a night. So I got a little concession and did that and made college tuition. I got interested in law because when I had to wait for the train from 3:15 in the afternoon until six in the evening, I went to the courthouse to listen to the cases and learn what the people were doing.

Ralph Moody

I got through college in June of '40 and the war was raging in Europe. I was a member of the Alabama National Guard while in college. They paid one dollar a week for drill. I remember when the war started for us. It was Sunday afternoon and we were in the theater at Fort Monmouth, New Jersey, at Signal Corps School. They announced that Pearl Harbor had been attacked, and Bob Hope, who was putting on a show, said, "Everybody get back to the barracks. We don't know what's going to happen." So we missed part of the Bob Hope show. Everybody was uptight.

I finished Officer Candidate School on 6 January 1942 as a second lieutenant. I got routine promotions and was a captain and adjutant to the regimental commander at the time I went overseas in 1944, and was executive officer of a signal heavy construction battalion. We went over on the Queen Mary. The troops were sleeping in the swimming pools. They had been drained, of course. We didn't have an escort because we were zigzagging so fast. We landed in Glasgow, Scotland, went down to Liverpool and stayed there until February of '45. Then we followed Patton's army into Germany. In June or July we got orders to go directly to Japan. We got on a boat sometime in August of '45 and while we were in route, before we got to the Panama Canal, the Japanese surrendered.

Back in New Jersey I started looking for a job. I'd been away from home for twelve years, so I decided to go down to Washington, D.C. and see if there were any government jobs open. I found out there was a job as attorney/investigator for the Office of Price Administration which was still in effect after the war. They had an opening in Honolulu and in Alaska. I'd never been to Hawaii, but I'd heard lots about it. I'd never been to Alaska and hadn't heard much about it. So I said I'd like to have the job in Honolulu. It turned out that that one'd been taken so I took Anchorage.

I came up here on Pan American. I went to Juneau for a two-week training period in what you were supposed to do and how you were supposed to do it. While in training, I met a lady who was also in training, and told her I was an attorney and would like to get into legal work and that this was the only thing I could get. She said, "Oh, I have a friend who is manager of the real estate department of the U.S. Corps of Engineers and they need an attorney, would you be interested?" I took the job with the understanding that I'd work for two weeks at the Office of Price Administration, until I could give notice and ask for a

Ralph Moody

141

transfer. Later I met the U.S. attorney, Raymond Plummer, and told him I was interested in getting a job with that office, which I did. I worked as an assistant for the U.S. Attorney's Office from '47 to '51 in the Anchorage office.

Then I decided to go into private practice with Wendell Kay and Paul Robison. They both got elected to the legislature and I was left with the law clerk. So I said, "Hey, if I'm going to do all this work, I might as well get my own firm." So I opened up my own practice right across from the old courthouse and practiced there until I became Alaska Attorney General in 1960. In the meantime, I was elected to the territorial legislature as the senator-at-large in the third judicial district which went from the Aleutian Chain to the Canadian border, and Yakutat almost to Mt. McKinley. I was chairman of the Senate Judiciary Committee in the territorial legislature. They established the legislative council then because we were trying to get statehood and wanted to be prepared, and I was appointed chairman of the council.

I served as legislative council chairman and senate judiciary committee chairman in the first state legislature and was majority leader in the first state senate. I remained on the legislative council until I was appointed by Governor Egan as attorney general and I served as attorney general from April 1960. Then Egan appointed me to the superior court bench in June of '62, and I stayed there for twenty-three years.

I handled a number of significant cases, I guess. The most well-known would be the longevity bonus/Zobel case. You know, people would be so mad, my court system staff would ask me to go home early so I wouldn't be harrassed. Then, I guess the next one was the election case in 1978 with Walter Hickel, Jay Hammond and Chancy Croft. Hammond won by ninety-three votes. I ruled that they should hold another election. Our supreme court overruled me, but I still think I was right. But really, I think probably the most rewarding part of being a judge is you get to see and feel the pulse of the community and the state everyday that you're on the bench. And something new and different keeps you alert.

When I decide a case, I call them like I see them. I've heard since I retired that I had the reputation of "shooting from the hip." Well, that's not necessarily true. You hear the evidence and you're not going to be any smarter waiting two weeks or two months. You wait that long and you forget what you've heard. After about three or four years on the bench, I realized, "Hey, I'm not going to get any smarter by sitting on this. If I've heard all the evidence, unless I need to look up some law, I'm ready to give a decision." Now, I don't think that's "shooting from the hip." Attorneys used to come in and say they thought I was wrong, that they'd have to take this to the supreme court. I'd say, "Well, go get the elevator to the fifth floor. That's what they're up there for and we've got to keep 'em busy." I also said that the supreme court is not necessarily right, they're just the final decision.

I think my philosophy has been to do what I think is right based upon the laws and rules and regulations in society. The only way we can have a meaningful society is to have rules and regulations. If you don't have rules, you don't have society. That means laws - guidelines for people to follow. If you don't follow them, you're going to have chaos and that's one of the things that's happening to society today. There may be too many rules and regulations; I'm not saying that you should have more. What happens is we so strictly interpret the rules that we let people slip by rather than saying, "Common sense says you stepped over the line a long time ago." It's really hard to define, but you have to have people who are willing to be guided by majority rule is what it amounts to.

I feel that integrity and honesty in what you're doing matters most. You have to have compassion, but if you think you're doing right, what is compassion for one person may be destroying someone else. I've always felt you have to do right; sometimes it hurts somebody, but you can't make the world over. I don't feel judges should make the law, but there should be a reasonable interpretation of it and I think through the recent years, there've been some rather peculiar interpretations.

Certainly people should have defense council, but I think we've gone too far. Once it's been determined that someone has committed a crime, we should forget many of the technicalities that let people out and create continued litigation.

We have safeguards in society. We have first the grand jury, then a jury who has to find guilty. If either one of them says no, you can't do anything about it. In addition, you have a judge who can sentence them. He can use his discretion. If the judge is wrong, you have the governor who can give a pardon. The courts here and everywhere are just overwhelmed with cases. There should be some changes made. There should be some finality. The supreme court ordinarily should be the final place, but many times lawyers fool around in the lower court with motions - and nobody's willing to accept a final opinion on anything. Everybody can make mistakes, we all agree, but I think we have to accept cedrtain principles. Do we let everybody go that's bad, because you might make a mistake on one person? If you find out you made a mistake, compensate them. But I don't think that justifies letting people go on and on. Something's wrong with society when they do that.

Ralph Moody
143

I'm really concerned with the proliferation of crime, not only in Alaska, but throughout the United States and possibly the world. I think the biggest problem is the breakdown of the family structure. And some way we've got to figure out some method of restoring a situation so one of the parents or a substitute parent is with the children, and that parents do what parents should do. And I think that's going to affect the whole structure of the state and the nation.

We have resources, if they're properly directed, to change things around. When you have a breakdown of the home, you're breaking down the morals, the basic principles of how people should live. If we don't get back to them, we're going to have serious problems.

One of the funniest things that happened when I was on the bench was that we started having attorneys come in wearing jeans and open shirts, and we felt like it wasn't appropriate to come in like that. So three judges in our court and a group from the bar got together and decided what was appropriate dress. One day, one of the male attorneys came in and he didn't have a tie on. So I said, "Mr. So and So, you don't have appropriate dress. You don't have a tie on. I'm going to recess and you bring fifty dollars and a tie back with you." In a few minutes he came back in with just kind of a shoestring tie. I looked down and he didn't have any shoestrings. And I said, "Well, I don't know if shoestrings are an appropriate tie, but I won't take issue with that. But you don't have any shoestrings now, so that'll be another fifty dollars until you get some shoe-strings."

Another time I was having trouble with attorneys forgetting their neck ties and I brought down some of my old ties that I'd had for forty years and hung them in the chamber. And if someone didn't have a tie, I'd say, "Hey, you forgot your tie, but I have an appropriate one for you. Come on back." It would be some outrageous tie. And I'd say, "Now I'm going to loan you this, but I want my tie back." Well, for a few days after that they'd come in and say, "Judge, I sure hope my tie's correct because I don't want to have to wear one of yours."

Fortunately, I've always had jobs that I liked and stayed there unless I saw something else which I felt I'd like better. I wouldn't take a job I didn't think I'd like because I think that's the worst situation you could have, even if the money's good.

Alaska's been wonderful to me from both a financial standpoint and that of personal satisfaction. I hope I have contributed something to Alaska; I've tried to. Most of my time has been in public life and I've tried to do it on the basis of what was good for most of Alaska and best for Alaska, and not any particular group of people.

Ralph Moody

Up here, we were a new state from the standpoint of law. We had a new constitution and our conditions and way of life and way of making a living were different. In many instances, I think you have to interpret law in light of the conditions in which you live. I had to call it as I saw it and there was no precedent for many of the things up here. I think it was unique and a privilege to be growing up with Alaska during the final days of the territorial setup and transition - to be in a growing community and environment.

I've never regretted it a day, coming here. I've never had any desire to go back. I don't know whether I've grown on the state, but the state has certainly grown on me. I enjoyed every bit of it. I would like to feel that I gained the respect of the people that I worked with, with them realizing and forgiving me for the mistakes I made as I forgive them for the mistakes I think they made.

Ralph Moody at his office - Anchorage, Alaska December 1984
Anchorage Daily News photo by Fran Durner

Ralph Moody

Sylvia Kobayashi

Anchorage - Sylvia sits intently while we paint and talk in her dining room. She is a small woman with lots of energy and determination.

The early years of my childhood conjure up painful recollections of hardship and misery. My father died several months before I was born. Life was very difficult for my mother. My remembrance of her is that she was always crying. She felt she had had a much better life in Japan but she could not afford to go back. This was in Seattle during the Depression years. I used to roller skate in the area where the King Dome is now. When I started school I couldn't speak a word of English. The schools were about ninety or ninety-five percent Japanese Americans because we were all clustered in that ethnic community area. So we were chattering away in Japanese when we were in kindergarten on up until the third grade.

When the war came, Pearl Harbor, I was a teenager. We heard the news over the radio and were just devastated. My brother, who is ten years older than I, was supporting the family by working two jobs and was very disillusioned because he was just getting to the point where he felt he was progressing financially. We were in the early group to be removed to the detention camp set up at the fairgrounds at Puyallup, Washington, in 1942. I was confused. We were American citizens but we were rounded up like cattle, corralled and fenced in by barbed wire with armed military guards. I was brought up to be one hundred percent American and I felt that I was. At school we proudly sang the Star Spangled Banner and saluted the American flag. We were obedient, loyal Americans and then to find ourselves in prison - it was something we just could not comprehend. Apparently, the United States did not want us and Japan considered us enemies. I don't recall any reasonable explanation given to us.

It was shocking to be lined up for everything, to be placed in one wooden room with bare floors and no furniture and many knotholes in the walls, and lining up for meals at the mess hall. Everyone was in a state of confusion. One night we all had food poisoning from the vienna sausage served for dinner. I was

Sylvia in southern California, 1947
Collection of the Kobayashi family

Koby with son Gary, 1954
Collection of the Kobayashi family

very sick and people were lined up at the latrines for a block. I will never eat vienna sausage again. My salvation was my youth. When you are young, problems may be incomprehensible but you tend to still have a spirit of optimism. Older people lose this when they are placed in that type of situation. They had worked all their lives to build up a nest egg only to see their dreams just disappear in one day.

We stayed in Puyallup for many months. And when it rained, as it does in Washington, everything turned to mud. But, we were eventually put on the train and sent to permanent camps at Minodoka, Idaho. We arrived in a dust storm and I found myself in a barren desert with clouds of dust everywhere and tar-papered buildings that would be our next home.

Born and raised in the Pacific Northwest, we were not accustomed to the hot, dry summer and very dry, cold winter. Each room had a pot-belied stove that heated the room. It was just a single room and no kitchen because we all ate in the mess hall. That was life in Minidoka. During harvest season there was a call for labor in the sugar beet fields and tomato canneries in Idaho and Utah. Young people were encouraged to sign up so I went out to work. We slept in itinerant camps. It was an opportunity to get out of camp and we were able to keep the money we made. Later, the government realized that it would be best for everyone concerned if we could be relocated. We were still not allowed to go to the West coast. However, the government encouraged the young people to leave camp and relocate and try to pick up our lives where we had left off. This was during the war. They realized that we are used to being productive and are not the type to just sit and do nothing which is contrary to our nature. It was also becoming very costly to maintain the camps.

The young people who could afford it were being accepted at colleges in the

Sylvia Kobayashi
148

Midwest and on the East coast. However, if one was not going to school then one had to have guaranteed employment in order to leave the camp. My girlfriend and I were hired out as domestics. She was the upstairs maid and I was the downstairs maid. We tried that for awhile but, as we could not have the same day off, this was not good for us. It was the first time we had left home and it was such a new experience for us we needed to be together constantly. Then we found a job sewing uniforms at a knitting company in Minneapolis on the night shift. We never told our parents we were working nights - our parents were still in the camp - but we were able to send money home on a regular basis.

I met Koby in Minneapolis. He was attending the Military Intelligence Language School for Japanese-American boys at Fort Snelling. He was sent to learn Japanese. He couldn't read or write Japanese and could barely speak the language. However, in nine months of intensive studying, he graduated as an interrogator/translator and was eventually sent to the Phillippines and to Japan after V-J day. I wrote to him almost daily.

I used to go to the movies a lot. I used to dream and look at the world through rose-colored glasses. I had my whole life ahead of me and I wanted to make my dreams come true. I just brushed aside those years of internment and evacuation. It was just something that happened that I didn't want to remember.

When Koby came back from the war in February 1946, he went home to southern California to help his family. He was very anxious to see how his parents were and how the business was. He and his brothers, who had fought in Europe with the 442nd Regiment, returned to find the family home in ashes. Everything of value had been stolen including their grand piano. The family farming and trucking businesses were gone. Everything was gone but the barren land.

Camp Minidoka in Idaho, 1942
Collection of National Archives - 210-GA-795 (National Japanese American Historical Society)
Francis Stewart photo

Koby came up in August of 1946 and we were married at the courthouse in Seattle. He took me home to the Kobayashi ranch in the desert country of southern California. Although the family home and businesses were in ruin, their spirit was still vibrant. Mother Kobayashi said, "From ashes we can build again." However, they never recovered from their financial and business losses.

It was a bad time to get married. Everyone was busy building the house and rebuilding the business. We lived with the family. The boys went off to work every morning and I stayed home. I learned a great deal from my mother-in-law during that time. Eventually we found an old quonset hut for ourselves. We didn't have a car and we didn't have any money and my husband worked seven days a week. I wanted to go to school but I had no transportation.

Then we moved to Los Angeles. I had to work as Koby was struggling to get back into the trucking business. It was very difficult for veterans to earn a living. I wanted him to go to school but he said he'd had enough of school in the army. When we had our child, I would take him, diapers and all, and ride in the truck with Koby. We were penniless but we had each other and we enjoyed being together. Koby was on the road much of the time. He worked seven days a week when there was work and worked himself ragged. There was too much competition in his business and I didn't care for southern California.

Then one day, out of a clear blue sky, my brother Tom came down from Alaska and offered my husband a job in Anchorage. I always wanted to go to Alaska, but Koby didn't want to. He had experienced cold in Minnesota and he didn't like it. And he had never worked for anyone in his whole life and here he would be working for my brother. Plus it was a big sacrifice because his truck was all paid for, a big diesel rig pulling a refrigerator van, and he felt he had a future in what he was doing. But I didn't, and I wanted to come to Alaska. I guess I meant more to him and we sold everything including the dog and the lawnmower, and moved up to Anchorage in December of 1965.

The first thing that Koby did was to buy a pickup and put a camper shell on it and we would go off every weekend and explore Alaska. It was wonderful in those days. We bounced around on the highway and just stopped off whenever we were ready to spend the night.

Later on I accepted a position at the Alaska Native Medical Center as a budget analyst. It wasn't long before I was paged to go to Emergency as they needed someone to interpret. At the time, I was extremely hesitant because I had not used the Japanese language for a number of years and I didn't know how much help I could be. But when I saw the patient, who was in pain and frightened beyond words, I immediately spoke a few words of Japanese. Just to see the joy in his eyes and his face lighting up was a wonderful experience for me, and I followed that patient until he was discharged from hospital. At that time there was no Japanese consulate in Anchorage. Having me on staff was very convenient for the doctors and nurses as injured Japanese seamen were brought in frequently from the Bering Sea.

This was the beginning of my volunteer work to help Japanese citizens needing assistance. As Japan Air Lines sent families to Anchorage for tour of duty station, my husband and I were able to help many adjust to a new way of life.

In 1972, my husband was injured in a work accident. He fell from a high elevation and struck his head and was unconscious for five days. That changed our whole life. He couldn't talk, he couldn't read, he couldn't write and was diagnosed as being disabled for life. But it is amazing what human determination can do. It took approximately five years, but he regained a good portion of his speech and he can read and write now. But it changed our whole way of living because my husband suddenly found himself confined to the house and I became the breadwinner. It was a very difficult time for us.

A few years ago I discovered that there was very little documentation about the history of the Japanese in Alaska. I knew that Japanese people had migrated to Alaska in the late 1800s and early 1900s, yet very little written material is available. I felt that this was a tragic situation and that someone should do something. I remembered when I was attending the University of California at Los Angeles, one of my early mentors was a U.S. history professor who was a social scientist. He had spent the war years teaching in an internment camp. He lectured for a whole hour on the internment of the Japanese Americans. In those days the history book contained one short paragraph about the Japanese Americans. What was shocking was that no one in the class knew that such an event had taken place.

So I decided that I would document the stories of the Japanese people in Alaska, how they struggled and what they contributed. I am also interested in the Aleuts who were removed from their home and interned during World War II as well as those from Attu who were taken prisoners to Japan.

So now I'm going to spend my time recording this history for future generations.

The move to Alaska changed my life. I'm doing things now that I never dreamed possible. When I came here, I knew I was home - the color of my skin or the shape of my eyes didn't matter.

Sylvia Kobayashi

Albert Yrjana

Ruby - Albert speaks very slowly, his Finnish accent adding a delightful cadence to the conversation. He's a shy man, who delights in the different perspectives in the sketches. He chooses one saying, "This here feller looks like he's been through some tough times."

They talk about Appalachia being in a bad way; well, it wouldn't hold a candle to upper Michigan. Because the logging, the mining, the traffic on the lakes, it all shut down during the Depression. '32 was the worst time. People that had some savings, they probably had spent most of them, and it was really a poor country there.

I was born on a small farm, seven miles west of Houghton, Michigan. My uncle had been to Alaska during the Gold Rush, and he had made a little stake, and wanted to get back to Alaska. He had a farm and family there in Michigan, so he couldn't. But he's the one that encouraged us young fellers to go to Alaska.

But the country was in a really bad way. The richest country in the world, with all that suffering some of the people had to go through before the welfare system got organized. I've seen it there in South Range, a small mining town, copper mining town, away from our farm. See, I come from my brother's farm on some spring work, and I was coming from there with the horse and wagon. And this feller, I gave him a ride. An Italian feller, and he had given the last two dollars and fifty cents to his wife and kids. Then he started to go make a round of the farms, to look for work or to get something to eat. That poor feller really suffered. The mines shut down. And the mines owned the grocery stores. And when you weren't working, you couldn't buy groceries. They wouldn't give you credit. So he was up against it. That's the way it was.

I tried to get to Alaska then. That was my pet dream. I was just a young feller, probably twenty-one, but in '32 I left home and I got as far as Wyoming. But the further I got west, the worse it was. You see I was out of my element. I knew working on farms, and logging and stuff like that, but that's cattle country. I didn't know how to ride a horse or rope a cow, so I had no chance of getting a job, because ranchers wouldn't take a greenhorn because there was

plenty of cowboys without jobs. And I had to turn back. But then in the winter of '34 it eased up a little, the Depression. Logging sort of started up again a little in Michigan, and I got a job at the logging camp. We put in eight hours on the job: not going to work or coming from it, we didn't get paid for that. And we got forty dollars a month, so that made it a little better than a dollar a day, for eight hours work. And you were glad to get it. Ten to fifteen men would call at the camp every weekend looking for jobs. And if you didn't put out, there was a man to take your place.

Then that winter, by saving every cent, I was able to save not quite a hundred dollars. And that's what I came to Alaska with. The government had already set up these soup kitchens. They had rented the low-priced hotels, and they'd give you a permit or slip that you could stay one night at the hotel and sleep, and get three meals. That was all through the northern states. It was some wise trick of some government expert, to keep the unemployed - they called them hobos, but they weren't, they were the unemployed - moving so that they couldn't congregate in one town or make friends or start protests. You got three meals and a bed, and then you had to move to the next town. There'd be two hundred, three hundred people on the freight going east, same amount on the west. And we'd wave to one another. But you could travel all over the United States that way. I was coming through the northern states, and I got to Spokane.

From Spokane, I got to Seattle, right there on the waterfront, they had what they called Hooverville. It was the unemployed, and people out of work - they made all kinds of shacks, whatever, to have a place to stay in. And you could even get a letter sent to Hooverville. But after times got better, they destroyed Hooverville. But that was where the unemployed had their own little community, there on the waterfront. See, the Finns, they're clannish as hell, and I'd go wherever I'd see a Finnish name or hear the language spoken. I got to talking with them, because most of them had been to Alaska. They're fisherman and loggers, anyhow. They always go back to that because it comes easy to any Finn. And some encouraged me to go to Alaska, and some would say to stay away from that mosquito-infested place.

But I come to Alaska anyhow. That was the time when everybody was out of work. You couldn't get a job, because everything shut down. I tried to get to Alaska when they were recruiting them colonists in Michigan and Minnesota. But I was a single man, and they wouldn't have me. Only families. But as it turned out, I got to Anchorage, and to Alaska, before the colonists come in '35. Then when the colonists come, then they had to get roads for those future

Albert Yrjana
154

farmers. So I worked in the Matanuska Valley, for the road commission which at the time was federal. Then they were building a road, from Tokatna to Nixon Fork, for the miners to haul their fuel. I worked on that. We built bridges along the little creeks. And I got a job on the road crew then. I stayed on it there two years before moving to the interior, to the mines, for higher pay. On the road commission, I got five dollars a day. Common labor was four dollars a day and room and board. But I knew how to pull a cross-cut saw and swing an axe, so I was rated as timberman, and I got five dollars a day. I stuck with it, until we heard of them big wages paid at the placer mines. I got a letter from one of the mine owners, saying that there's a job for me in Ophir if I come. Two hundred and forty dollars a month, and boy I made tracks quick. That would be in 1938. The first job I got at a placer mine was in Ophir, for Uotilla and Hard. They were the miners. And that was two hundred and forty dollars a month, so I was in the chips then. That beat anything I had ever had. From Ophir then I went to Cripple, what they call now Folger. And from there I moved to Ruby. There was some fellers from Ruby working at the mine in Cripple, and they told about a sawmill for sale there in Ruby. And me and my brothers, see, - I'd sent them the fare to come up - we had a little money saved up, so we went to take a look at the mill. And I bought it, 'cause it was cheap. We had to rebuild the whole darn thing. There were four of us. But two of them, after a year, that summer in Ruby, went back to Michigan. They were sorry that they left.

But the war came on then. And everybody had to sign. If you were healthy, you had to be in war work, or in the army. There was no alternative. The government signed up every mill that there was in the country. You had to saw for the government. They had to build these airfields. Lumber that was sawed at our mill in Ruby, come even into Fairbanks to this Ladd Field, or Eielson. They were short of lumber. And most of the lumber went to Galena from Ruby. Them buildings in Galena are from logs cut on the Nowitna River and sawed in our mill.

After the war, I got a job on the road commission there in Ruby and I trapped in the winter. I sold the mill, and then had to take it back because the guy didn't pay for it. It's now demolished. It was an old type steam-powered mill. It took twelve to fourteen men to run it.

With my brothers, we had a freighting outfit, and a sawmill. When they left, I couldn't handle the both of them. So I sold the sawmill and stuck with the freighting. But I should have kept the mill and let the freighting go. Because then there was a time there that mining was right down flat on its back. And during the war, no mining went on at all. You couldn't buy oil or parts. And

Albert Yrjana
155

Ruby in 1911
William and Margaret Taylor Collection of the University of Alaska Fairbanks Archives

young fellers had to be in war work. Only the old fellers were able to stay at their mines. But they couldn't get any parts or materials. It was tough. But they could do hand work and keep it going. But I put in twenty-six seasons with the highway department. I could have worked at their shop in the wintertime. I forget what they paid a month. But I could do just as well trapping. Not as big a paycheck every month, but after adding everything up, expenses here in Fairbanks, and what my expenses were in Ruby, I could do just as well trapping, be my own boss, and you don't have to go out in cold weather. When it's too cold you can stay in the cabin and keep the fire going, or cut the wood. And nothing moves in fifty below on the trapline. The animals are smarter than people anyhow. They'll just go under the snow and stay warm. As long as they don't get hungry. From below thirty-five, very little moves.

In the early days of Ruby it was still the pick and shovel era. The mines needed a lot of men and there had been a modern bathhouse for the miners there. Three women had run it. They had these big cast-iron tubs in there. They took care of the miners. I guess the women would have called it the "house of ill repute." But that's what they had for the men there. It had been quite a thing for the miners in the early days of Ruby. So it was quite a business, all right. After the pick and shovel era went out, and then the cats and draglines come in, the mines didn't need that many men anymore, so business went on the bum and they had moved out. The building is still up and we've used those bathtubs for duck ponds and stuff like that. We have the bath tubs in our garden right now. I wasn't in on the duck and goose business. All they need is just a mud puddle, they don't need deep water. But the wife thought the bath-

Albert Yrjana
156

tub would be the ticket for them. But there was no other use for them, there was no running water in any place in Ruby at that time.

The wife, Dolly, was born thirty-five miles out of Dawson, on a creek. That's where she grew up her first years, and then she went to school in Dawson. The church had a school there. Then the family moved to a small farm in Canada. But the British or the English didn't like the Germans, and her father was a German. So after eight years in Canada, they moved back to Alaska and stayed there the rest of their lives. I met her in Ruby, the winter of '39. The family had had a restaurant in Ruby, but the girls had given it up when their parents died. And one sister was the postmaster. Then in the summer they'd cook at the mining camps. When I got to Ruby, well, we got acquainted, as young fellers will. My brother married one of the girls, Dolly's sister.

Dolly'd run dogs all the time, since she was a kid. You had to have some dogs to pull your water up to the house from the river. We had to haul the water from the Yukon to the house. We were drinking Yukon water at that time. There was no wells, yet. But then when they built up this Ladd Field, and all this sewage from Fairbanks come down, we had to quit that, and dig wells in Ruby.   Then when I started trapping, well, we always had the dog team. Then I got hit with a car here in Fairbanks. That put an end to my trapping for six years. But I'm going to try it again this winter. Now I use snow machines. A dog team is an expensive thing, unless you have a fish camp. I fished there, we have a camp in Ruby, up about a mile and a half or so. I fished for fifteen years, just for ourselves, and even made salmon strips. You had to have a fish camp to keep a team of dogs. Otherwise you couldn't buy that much fish and stay solvent. You'd go broke.

We always have a garden and stuff grows there really good. Of course they've had a garden at our place since the

Front Street in Ruby, July 1912
W.F. Erskine Collection of the
University of Alaska Fairbanks Archives

Albert Yrjana
157

early days of Ruby. And I'm always adding more fertilizer to it. It's good soil, and it grows stuff.

What I like about Alaska is the freedom to move around. I don't care for town life. Heck, after you get to know the streets, and where the watering places are, and the theater and stuff, well that's all there is to know. Out in the woods, you're learning all the time. And it's a freer life.

You can turn to anything you wanted there in Ruby. I've always been outdoor-oriented. Hunting, fishing, trapping, it comes easy to a Finn because our ancestors had lived that way in Europe. So it's an inborn trait, or acquired, because you take to it, and you like it. If I were to go anywhere, I'd go further north. I'd like to go seal hunting. That Herbie Nayokpuk from Shishmaref - I have a standing invitation from him to come there in June and he'll take me out seal hunting. I met him when he was on this Iditarod run. I sold him wolf and wolverine skins. He had women in Shishmaref who would still do some sewing and I got a pair of his boots. They cost one hundred dollars all right, but I had to have them. I haven't worn them, but they're hanging in the attic. If I ever get to Shishmaref, I'll put those boots on, and I'll be one of the gang.

It was just a nice life for us. The wife had her gardening and dogs to take care of. And I had to work and earn a living. I worked summers for the road commission. It's a nice easy life, nothing hurry about it. I dabbled in mining a little. See, I had ground there all right, then I leased it out. The darn fellers that leased it, they're not honest. They were all from Fairbanks and Nenana. Well, they were crooks. First thing we knew, they were stealing the nuggets. We heard that one of the partners had been showing a big nugget here in Fairbanks, and trying to sell it. That's the first time we heard that they were crooked. We trusted them too much. The one that was running it, he was a crook from way back. It was after the accident and I couldn't move around except with two canes. I could drive a car or pickup all right, but I had to have two canes to walk with.

It's been six years since it happened now. But one thing it did make a change in me all right. I appreciate my friends and people better than I did. I was what you'd call fairly independent at that time. But laying there in the hospital, with people come to visit and check on me, by golly I liked it. I appreciate my friends more and my wife. She is the one that really had to put up with me. But now it's the other way around. She's helpless now with the stroke. But we're making it.

Heck, in Ruby you've got fish year 'round in the river, gardens grow good, and meat and fur in the woods. Where can you find a place like that? And then

Albert Yrjana
158

if you have a boat, you've got five rivers to run on. And the Yukon the sixth. Where is there another place like it? We've got the Big Creek, Deep Creek, Nowitna, Melozi and Yuki Rivers. All within two hours of home with any kind of a boat. You wouldn't find a place like that if you tried.

I didn't do any dog racing myself. But I used dogs for trapping. And they are still, for a trapper, the best thing, if he is really a professional trapper. A dog team still beats a snow machine. Because, you got no gas troubles, no spark plug troubles. When you tell them to go, they go. You make your rounds like I did beaver trapping. See, I'd be out all day, going from one beaver house or lodge to another and they learn the routine. There's nothing to it. You do your work; you check your sets and if you have beaver in your sets, well then you load them into the toboggan and away you go to the next set. They get to know the darn game, and they're in it as much as you are. You wouldn't cover as much ground, but then, what is trapping? It's just miles and observation. If you go too fast, you miss more than you catch up with. A dog team is still the best, if you have a good team. A poor team, that's a nuisance, but a good dog team, they'll take you around and do it for the fun of it.

Trapping to me is still important. Heck, it's a way of life. If you know your trapping, you're not dependent on anyone and you're more independent the more you know. Your food is there, you always have something to eat, if you know how to go get it, and your wood and fire to keep warm with. I like it.

What changed Alaska altogether is the oil companies. They get their oil too cheap. It was a better life in Alaska before, because everyone worked to earn their living. And they were more honest than they are now.

It's changed altogether from what it was them early days. But not all for the best. When I first come to Ruby, there was two stores there, the N. C. Company and Carl Bohn. And if you didn't like one store, you could go to the other. Now we have only one, and they can charge whatever prices they want. There's no competition. The people are different now. See, Ruby is a welfare town now. It was miners, trappers, fishermen and workmen. Now what we have there in Ruby, welfare is so high, that it doesn't pay a lot of them to go out trapping. They might as well stay in town. But it's ruining the people. Just too easy a living.

At eighty-one going on eighty-two, you have lived most of your life already. When I first come into the country, my life span was that long [three feet]. It's now down to this [three inches]. I'm going to try to get three wolverine this winter. I don't know of anyone that'll even come close to my record, fifty.

Albert Yrjana
159

George Rogers

Juneau - The books, prints, and music that surround us in their home reflect the many aspects of their lives - and he talks of Juneau and his involvement with Perseverance Theatre.

Jean and I came to Alaska January 7, 1945, and in a sense it was the beginning of our real life. We'd been married about two-and-one-half years and we were seeking new worlds to conquer.

Meeting Jean was one of the most meaningful things in my life and it still is. When we came together at Berkeley it was as if we had prepared as children to meet each other, to be together. Like two streams coming together, it's difficult to separate us. When you talk about me, you're talking about Jean, and the same is true of Jean. Above everything else, this has been the big thing. Another has been the decision to stay in Alaska. I was directed to come to Alaska but we made the decision to stay.

Alaska fit my professional dreams perfectly. It was an island, in a sense, politically and geographically - a territory with about seventy-nine thousand people.

I came up here originally with the Office of Price Administration. Due to bad vision, I was 4-F during World War II. My "war duty" was with the Office of Price Administration, trying to control inflation during the war and working on fish prices. It was a quixotic sort of enterprise, trying to regulate fishermen. Ernest Gruening urged me to stay on, and after serving with him for two years I went back to Harvard to get my Ph.D.

Gruening was preparing Alaska for statehood. So one of my first assignments was to design a revenue system for the territory. There wasn't any worthy of the name, it was a holdover from Gold Rush days, a series of taxes on dance halls, local breweries which didn't exist any longer, undertakers, a crazy patchwork. Ernest Gruening's motto was that without taxes you don't have civilization. And I believe in that too. What Gruening wanted was an income tax, a statewide property tax and a business license tax. I worked out the three of them. The property tax was not upheld by the courts but the other two were.

Early Juneau circa 1949
Collection: Early Prints of Alaska, Photo No: 01-2230, Alaska State Library

They became the basis of the tax system.

The next step was organizing programs, so we could have the skeleton of a state government before we became a state. This all culminated in 1956 with the two-year Constitutional Convention at Fairbanks. This was one of Ernest Gruening's strategies - to not wait for Congress, but to get the constitution ratified by the people of Alaska, elect two senators and a representative, have them go back to Washington, D.C., present themselves in Congress and say, "We are here to be seated." And it worked.

I participated in that as an active secretary for the first month, then I was a consultant and a source person. So I had the feeling of being there at the creation.

Ever since then, it's been a succession of things like that in my career. I've had the opportunity of not only observing dramatic change - political, social, and economic - but being part of it. And in the meantime, Jean and I have been working together creating a home. One of the first things we did was to start building the house we're living in now and building a family. We eventually had six children, all adopted.

Aristotle said that a community had to be limited to a size that when all the members were assembled in one place, the human voice, a speaker in the center, could reach all of them. It has to be something in which the members can interact, with access to one another. If it got beyond that sort of communication level, then you had to create another community. Right now I feel Juneau

George Rogers
162

is about the optimum size. Anchorage is beyond what I consider optimum, Fairbanks is several communities and each one has its own orientation and its own life and they somehow interact. And this is what I think has happened to our civilization. We've gone beyond human scale too many times. The human scale has been increased tremendously since the ancient Greeks who had to shout to be heard. Now you have your voice augmented, you have television, you create a larger community. But we haven't mastered that yet. The technology is there, but somehow we haven't put it together.

A community is not a monolithic uniformity. Vitality has its base in diversity and a true community accommodates diversity and this translates into a vitality and vibrance which I find in Alaska, and in Juneau.

When I first hit Alaska I tried to make sense out of it. Alaskans are very ethnocentric - this is it and everything else is nowhere. I had to have some sort of a framework and my first basis for analysis was a geographic one. It was like a loom; the warp was geography, the weft was history. Alaska is a product of both those forces. The geography determines regional and local physical units; the history determines points of view. I divided them arbitrarily. Native Alaska, represents subsistence, self-sufficient systems in harmony with the environment. The colonial, which came in first with the Russians, later with the New England whalers and everybody else, looks upon Alaska as simply a warehouse from which you just wrench certain resources - just take what you want and forget the rest of it. That view's still with us. And then you move into the military/defense Alaska which is a recognition of geographic location. That's the reason Seward engineered the purchase of Alaska - not for its resources, but because you could control the whole North Pacific, in theory, by having your naval forces there.

After statehood I saw that a new type of Alaska was emerging which combined many of these things but which went beyond. It was colonial, but with the understanding that Alaska was a place where people would live as well as make a living. That this would be home.

Another part of both our lives has been the sense of a frontier. It's a cliche that Alaska's the last frontier. That's a lot of hogwash in many respects. Alaska is mid-America when you get into Anchorage and to a certain extent in Juneau and Fairbanks. But to make your life, you have to have a sense of pushing beyond boundaries. This is something that has also been a part of our lives. Jean and I as students at Berkeley took part in the first interracial experiment in the East Bay, the church where you had a black and a white pastor, a mixed congregation living together, worshipping together, doing things together. That's

George Rogers
163

the sort of thing we've been pushing always through our lives. Alaska's a good place to get into that.

Both Jean and I were always into social service. Doing things not for ourselves but finding ourselves in helping others and working at things. We grew up in the Great Depression when there was a lot of experimentation with new forms of organizing enterprise. In those days you didn't run around and throw rocks through bank windows, you tried to change the system by creating alternate systems. It was the spirit of our time. All the thinking people and educators of young people were into that kind of thing. It was not unusual. It was the thing to do.

I graduated from high school in 1934. My father had had only intermittent employment and I had two younger brothers, and after three months of hard searching, I landed a job with Standard Oil of California and ended up in their economics department as a high school graduate.

In that department there wasn't one economist, which is why it was able to function so effectively. People in the department had been selected out of each section of the company. But we were dealing with the way the industry really operated, not the text book way it operated. There was illegal collusion between the seven major oil companies. Our job was to take the results of their meetings, put them together into what these days you would call a model, from which we then worked out what the interaction would be. So I got hands-on experience dealing with one of the big movers in the basic economy. But I was not comfortable with it because I could see loyalties were to the corporation, not to anything or anybody else, including the nation. Immediately before our entry into World War II, for example, we were getting around the munitions laws to continue exporting aviation fuel to Japan by manipulating the mix of products loaded on Japanese tankers. Then when all exports to Japan were terminated, trying to establish an avenue through Mexico, through a neutral country, to continue providing the Japanese with what they needed to wage war, which was against my principles.

By this time it was 1940, my father had a full-time job, and I had postponed my education for five-and-one-half years so I enrolled and got my degree in two-and-one-half years.

Choosing to go into economics was partly because of the Depression. My great love as a small child was art and architecture. I always dreamt of being an architect but it was obvious I wasn't going to get any work if I became an architect. It's hard for young people today to understand what happened. Everything came to a halt. My father was driven crazy because he was reduced to just

George Rogers
164

Early Juneau circa 1946
Collection: Early prints of Alaska, Photo No: 01-2831, Alaska State Library

maybe one or two days a week working and had a family. In those days there were no social programs, no relief programs. There was no concept that anything was wrong with the system and yet the system was not functioning and hadn't been functioning for several years and I just decided I had to do something.

I've always tested myself. My great fear is vegetating. I feel that your life is enriched by going beyond what you already know, what you can already do, and trying something more. Trying to do something beyond that. You push yourself. You go to the limits or beyond the limits. You have to have this feeling that accomplishment is one of the great "highs"; being a part of something, creating something, or doing something where there's a breakthrough at a higher level. I'm a great believer in imagination as well as intelligence. Intelligence is O.K., but imagination is much more important in our lives and also in survival of society.

Once I'd started academic training, a Ph.D was my minimum goal, but going to university at Berkeley and Harvard were not high points, they were a validation of what I was trying to do. A high point was the Fellowship I had to Cambridge - it was an exposure to a whole new world, a whole new way of looking at life. Exposure to magnificent libraries, research materials, exposure to people who were doing original things in a way that I didn't find at Harvard and at Berkeley.

One of Parkinson's laws is when anything becomes well organized, it's dead. I think that's very true. It's true of institutions, it's true of systems and

George Rogers
165

George Rogers
Anchorage Daily News photo

it's true of people whose lives become too organized. Things have to be in a state of disorganization, a state of evolving. At Cambridge I found a new way of looking at education. Their whole educational system is very flexible, it's almost tailored to the individual student, with a tutorial system. You do have certain requirements, but you're not stuck with a catalog that says you have to take so many credits of this and that and take it in this particular context.

Society has become fragmented. It has lost its sense of a center and direction. It's not giving enough recognition to the importance of the small parts of the system. Like in a play, there are no small parts. And the same thing is true of society as a whole, where all the bit players are critically important.

Society has become dehumanized and it's because we haven't done what the founding fathers did, which was to find a way of coping with the new scale. I don't have the answer, but we need to focus on that sort of thing - a republic made up of sovereign states that surrender a certain part of their sovereignty into a union, which then is still able to create. Community provides a center, the base, and this has to be rediscovered, redeveloped now. There are many attempts being done on this in small scales. One is to revolt against centralization.

With everything around us seeming to disintegrate and fall apart, I think what we as individuals can do is try to make some sort of meaning out of our own lives, our own surroundings. We can't really do anything about the greater thing until we do something about ourselves. You maybe are not able to overcome your adversaries, but you can prevent them from doing things to you that destroy your meaning. Voltaire said in Candide that the most we can do is tend our own gardens and observe the passing scene. We can do more, but I think we should start with that. Tend our own little gardens, make them flourish, make them grow and be lovely and then work from that. But we have to start somewhere, start with ourselves, start with our local community, start with our state and then move on.

This bear is a yearly visitor at the Rogers home.

George Rogers

167

Natalie Simeonoff

Kodiak has a restlessness inherent in many fishing villages. But secure in Natalie's kitchen, we have fresh corn bread, more salmon, and tea, and we talk.

Woody Island is easterly from Kodiak, and all of us children were born there. The island has a great deal of history because from there the A.C. (Alaska Commercial) Company shipped ice out to San Francisco. This was probably during the late 1800s, and they employed a lot of Natives. At the time of my birth there were about ten families living over there. A mixture of Aleut and Russian.

There were nine of us kids and I was next to the eldest. When our family was still small, we used to make the trips to summer fish camps by *bidarky*. There would be Mama, my sister and I, usually a cat and a dog and possibly a hen or two all tucked inside the waterproof covering. This is probably where my claustrophobia comes from as we travelled at least twenty or thirty miles.

Everything was shank's mare. You rowed wherever you went. The men used their *bidarkies*, but by the time I was growing up there were maybe one or two in existence, so we used dories. When Kelly and I were first married, we used to row back and forth to Kodiak and get our groceries and when Kelly wasn't home, the children and I came. But you didn't think anything of it. When I was a child, because salmon was one of our principal sources of food, our whole village would get together and row over to what is now called Buskin River and the airport. It was then an experimental station and sheep ranch. We would camp right there on the banks of the river and proceed to salt and dry our fish for the coming winter.

And I remember what a holiday mood it was. As a little, tiny girl, one of my earliest memories is being out there late after everyone had left. We were drying our fish and it started to rain. And it rained and rained and rained. And I remember us walking in. Papa carried me on top of a five-gallon can he strapped to his back and we were drenched. Mama was carrying my older sister Nastia. And they walked from the ranch all the way into Kodiak, a distance of five miles.

When she married, my mother moved from the Kodiak Baptist Mission,

where she had been totally cared for, into a completely Native way of living where they moved from fish camp to fish camp. Mama was kind of a pet with the people of the mission. She could sew very well, knit, crochet, and cook. The Mission Society shipped up boxes and boxes of materials and clothing, and Mama would take the old coats and make jackets for the children out of them. I don't believe I ever had a boughten coat, but we were perfectly happy because we all could sew. We learned to spin yarn. As the sheep at the sheep ranch wandered around, their fleece would get stuck on the bushes. We would pick bags of this and then take it home. Mama would wash it and card it, and then we'd spin it. And when the men's socks wore out we'd just rip out the bottom and knit in a new pair of feet. In the evenings we would either cut rags for rugs, darn, knit, crochet, or spin.

These are the things I found marvellous about my mother. From a protected, sheltered life at the mission, she went into another culture completely and did well, learning to speak the languages. She was from Sand Point and had spoken the western Aleut dialect before she came here, and then spoke English all those years until she was eighteen or nineteen years old, and then moved into another culture and learned to speak a new Aleut dialect as well as all the things that a person needed to do for survival. She also spoke Russian fluently.

We children had a three-way learning thing all the time. We went to school at an English-speaking school. In the Native area, we went off to the fishing grounds and were with our own people and spoke Aleut. Papa was very Native, but his father was a Russian, so we had the Baptist influence, we had the Native, which we lived, and then we had the Russian influence because we went to the Russian Orthodox Church.

On the island there was only seven or eight of us children who played together because the children at the mission were kept within the confines of the mission and not allowed to fraternize with us except under school conditions. We were Natives and they were not. Looking back, I see how they were very patronizing. And the Baptist Mission land was the choice land on Woody Island. The workers got select pieces of land because they knew the way to do it, they knew the system and we didn't. In fact, we never did get title to our property on Woody Island.

Mama was self-educated. She probably went through the eighth grade and that was it. She read to us all the time. She would get books from the mission library and read. Mama didn't have an easy life by any means. Papa abused her and she finally left him after twenty-five years of marriage. Several years later she married our stepfather. There were nine of us kids and he made sure that

Natalie Simeonoff

Natalie's stepfather, Mike, (on the right) with the Baptist superintendant at the mission shop

Natalie at fourteen on Woody Island

Natalie standing in the back on the right with her sisters, 1927

All photos are the collection of Natalie Simeonoff

we ate, had shoes on our feet, and that we had something at Christmas time. He was good to us.

We lived on game, seal, ducks, fish, beans, and the potatoes that we grew. Mama did everything. From a whole seal she would flesh it, get all the fat off because the fat was important. Then she'd take the stomach and flesh it so that there was just the membrane left and wash it very clean, tie the bottom end and inflate it. She'd hang it on the clothsline until it dried. Then she'd take the fat and cut it in strips, just keep a continuous cut, then stuff it in the neck until the bag was full and hang it in the *sarai* which is a shed. During the course of winter it would marinate and all that would be left would be the oil which we used on boiled cod fish and salt salmon.

We always looked forward to the times when we could get seal. The hunters never could get any except in the spring when they'd get two so we'd have enough oil to last all winter long. In earlier years, we'd have whale blubber too. The stores sold whale blubber up until I was about ten or fifteen years old. The whalers would just anchor up right in the Kodiak harbor and they'd be flenching their whales and rendering out the fat and the blubber and they also gave the mission a lot of the meat, too.

We had a tremendous religious upbringing because Papa was a *Starosta* which is a steward of the Russian Orthodox Church. He took care of the books and the candles and things like that. We celebrated Russian Christmas, which is removed from the American version by two weeks and is on the seventh of January by the Julian calendar.

One of the celebrations that we used to enjoy so much was masquerading after Christmas. It is represented as the time that Herod was searching for the baby Jesus and the people did everything to foil his attempts. We masqueraded for a week. We would go to houses, to our friend's places, and they would try to guess who we were. We used to believe the old story about the master of the house who was talking to the people masquerading and went over to feel them and found nothing but straw. They weren't real people, they were beings from some other phase.

Everything came to a kind of a climax on Russian New Year's Eve and if it didn't hit on Saturday, they could have a great big dance and a real big celebration. Our Russian Orthodox Sabbath started on Friday night or Friday morning, so we didn't ever dance on Saturday, but we could dance on Sunday. One person would devote their living room and maybe one bedroom to having the dances there. I remember they used to have these kerosene lamps which reflect along the wall. We had phonographs and if we were lucky we'd get somebody

Natalie Simeonoff

Russian Orthodox Church
Collection of the Kodiak Historical Society

that could play a guitar and a mouth harp and they would have a dance every night until about midnight and everybody danced. The children danced too.

And this went on for a week until they finally celebrated Russian New Year. Then the people would make someone represent the Old Year. They'd dress him in rags and they'd play music and dance around the hall and hop around. Then they'd take the Old Year down and throw him into the sea to wash off the evil spirits. You can imagine in January how cold it was. They'd throw the Old Year

Natalie Simeonoff

Natalie harvesting potatoes with her parents, 1929

out and then the New Year would come parading in. Normally, you think of the New Year as being dressed in a diaper and having a big swath of gilt and things, but the Natives in their naivete' would dress him up as Uncle Sam. Often times after this celebration, they would all go and jump in the sea to wash the evil spirits away. Our father acted the part of the Old Year once but because we children cried so much, they didn't dunk him.

The Russians taught the Natives a lot of good things. One was to use kelp for our gardens. And kelp is wonderful. It warms the soil and makes it pliable. All of our gardens had a southern exposure. Our gardens, the Fadaoff family gardens, were two or three miles from our home. In the morning, Mama would put together a lunch and get the baby ready, and Mama and I, and Nastia, Julia, and the baby would trot over the hills to garden. Papa would get the dory and he would row around to where we were going. The gardens were right next to the water, up on the bank, because you had to have the proximity of the kelp beds. We would spend several days like this. Papa would dig the garden first and then we'd start the raking and setting up for the beds. He would go out with a dory and pick up the kelp, get the dory loaded and bring it ashore. We had a carrier that in Russian they call a *nosilka*. It's a big box with handles and one person can stand abreast and hold it, and then another person can stand in the back and hold it, and you'd trot along.

Being the oldest ones in the family, we always fell to the heavy work, my sister and I, getting the water, and carrying the *nosilka* up the hill with all this kelp in it. Everybody was making gardens so there wasn't anybody else to help Papa do it. Mama would be working; she'd be doing the raking with the baby tied to her back; Papa would be getting the kelp; and Nastia and I would be carrying the *nosilka* up the hill. We raised enough potatoes in this garden to last all winter for a family of maybe six people.

When I was thirteen years old, I started to work as a maid here for the Kraft family, one of the only five non-native families in Kodiak. And here comes masquerading time with a big dance hall and wonderful music to dance to. I was fifteen and one-half. Kelly was at the dance and we fell in love. And I've been in love with him ever since.

I was always so grateful that I married one of my own kind. There were no cultural differences. We liked the same things and we understand the Native way of life. I'm not saying that we had a hard time, but a Native was a second-class citizen. But I always taught my children that just because you're a Native doesn't mean you have to be a second class citizen and don't hesitate to say you're a Native.

After I married Kelly in '35 or '36, we built our home over there on Woody Island, close to where my mother lived. It was a wonderful place to live. All the children loved it. There must have been a hundred and some odd people and our children went to school there and the high school children commuted on the boat every day to town. In 1940, after the war was over, we moved over to Kodiak so Kelly could work. Then in 1948, we found that we could buy our old house back on the island and if we moved over there they would have enough children to start a school. So we moved back and it was a heavenly time. We stayed over there until about 1956. Kelly was working for FAA and at that time under the Eisenhower administration you couldn't take any summer leave, which would mean he couldn't fish. So he quit and went fishing. We didn't want to leave the island. But Kelly had to work and the only work was crab fishing so finally we just gave in and moved back in to a home here in Kodiak that we had bought.

So then it started the struggle. You know, with fishing, it's chicken one day and feathers the next. There's no happy medium.

When statehood was declared in 1959, we voted out fish traps. Big companies owned these huge traps. Our people had worked at gill net sites where you anchor a net on the shore and then out at sea and you go out and pick your nets two or three times a day. That livelihood was almost wiped out with the advent of fish traps because the fish traps caught thousands of salmon. When they were abolished, we were able to gill net again. So Kelly picked out a site that he wanted at Uganik. We went out fishing for the summer and agreed to take on the winter watchman's job at one of the canneries. About fourteen miles from the cannery, we built a home that we call "Cottonwood." We now own the property. Our grandchildren by then were big enough to walk around and our children would always make a special trip and come out. We'd spend Christmas together or they would come and spend all summer.

There always were bears there. They broke into our house twice in Uganik. We had to make the house shipshape, because we'd leave it every winter for

Natalie Simeonoff
175

three or four months. The first time the bears broke in they did some damage, but not irreparable. The next year they broke in again and this time if we hadn't come back home they would have literally torn that house apart. They tore the door off the refrigerator. They knocked the doors in and some of the windows. They took the bedding and carried it outdoors. They literally destroyed every bit of the food. They broke into the cans, a five-gallon can of salad oil, a thirty-gallon keg of butter, one hundred pound sacks of sugar and flour. There were bloody nose prints on the ceiling because of them tearing the cans. That house had to be literally redone.

It must have been '74 when we moved back in to Kodiak. By that time our son Freddie had been killed in Vietnam and our son Peter was dead. I suppose we all think that we're invincible, but when I look back on it, we never thought of the imminence of losing one in the family. Even when Freddie went to Officer's Training School and was a helicopter pilot, I never thought that he would be killed. And then he was only over there a few short weeks and he was killed. Then Peter was just devastated and he died two years afterward. And I couldn't stay out there. There were too many memories.

It was then that I went to work at our Native association. I went to work for seven hundred and fifty dollars a month as a health career counselor. I was grateful for the chance to try some other type of thing and by the time I finished, five years from then, I was the health director and my salary was about twenty-five thousand a year. But I'd worked myself up to the point where I'd reached the level of my own incompetence, the Peter Principle. I would have had to go back to school again. I love to learn, it gives you a new lease on life, and I was studying as much as I could, just cramming information into my brain. I would take every course that I could think of that would enhance my ability to grasp this, because this was big business.

But this was the thing I found deplorable about the Alaska Native Land Claims Settlement Act. It threw us into a completely different phase. We had to be corporate people, with no understanding of it. Fortunately, those of us that had a little bit more moxie could handle it, but I broke out with eczema because I was so harassed and so nervous over the work and the responsibility of being president of our corporation and being on the interim board of the profit corporation, wearing many, many hats, being on the Alaska Native Health Board, travelling back and forth to Anchorage and being completely in demand.

But one thing that the land claims did was bring the Native people together. It made a union of them.

One of the positive things, and that's happened just recently, is the fact

Natalie Simeonoff

that they're moving toward closing down alcohol in villages. That to me is one of the biggest things. I think that they were ready for this and they had to do it themselves. I never thought I'd see the day that this would happen, and it has.

But I was ready to quit. Kelly was retired and it was the right time.

I think the nice thing about my life is the fact that I enjoyed doing the things that to many other people would be a chore. I enjoyed going out and getting wood, rowing the skiff along and stopping where there was a big bunch and loading it into the boat. I loved working in the garden and sewing. We had to do things to supplement our income because we had seven children.

I think that the reverses just make you stronger. The best times of our lives were when we had some reverses. All of our smarts came to the fore. We immediately put our forces to work to go ahead and better our condition. We proved that we were perfectly capable of taking care of ourselves and doing a good job of it. Come hell or high water we could do it. I've proved to myself that I can work and I've dared to do a lot of things.

I look back on all of our time that we've lived and the places we've lived and they were all satisfying and good, outside of losing the boys. And even that I think is a part of life. Somebody asked me after Freddie was killed, "I suppose you hate the Vietnamese?" And I said, "No, I don't hate the Vietnamese, I don't hate anybody," I just, well, maybe hated God for awhile, because how could something like this happen to us. Losing a child is absolutely horrible, it's worse than death. You feel like burying yourself in sackcloth and ashes; you feel like grovelling because you are so grievously hurt and bereft. I don't think that anybody, no matter what kind of person they are, ever reconciles themselves to losing a child or a loved one. But time is a wonderful healer.

I think that we're here just by happenstance and life absolutely depends on what you make of it. If you're lucky, you grow to live to be seventy-five years old, like myself and hope to live to be ninety or one hundred. Anyway, that's what I'm aiming at. For me, I don't want to make a big splash or anything, but it's nice to be admired, it's nice to have people like you. But if they don't like me, I like me. I like the way I live and I think I'm a good person and to me that's very, very important. I think one of the things I would hate more than anything is to be misunderstood and thought of as devious, unkind, a liar or a cheat. I wanted mostly for my children to be good people and this is what they turned out to be.

Natalie Simeonoff

Spelling of place-names and rivers is taken from the
Dictionary of Alaska Place Names, U.S. Geological Professional Paper No. 567.

(p) after page number indicate photograph

182